Detour

A short story about a long journey

Jane Wirth

Detour

Dedication

This story is dedicated to all who experienced a moment in time that changed their life

Detour

Introduction

In August of 2007 I was diagnosed with Acute Lymphoblastic Leukemia. In one phone call my entire life changed, altered by no plan of my own. I began this story shortly after going through my initial treatment. Time passed and I let it go. 5 years later, I relapsed and was told I needed a bone marrow/stem cell transplant. I began writing again, using what I had already written and adding my current journey.

The writing of this story allowed me to process both my past experience and the one I am currently living. It is a story of hope, inspiration, and gratitude. It is also a story of working through fear, sadness and pain.

It is my sincere hope that *Detour* will inform, inspire, and help others to process their own "moment," or experiences that seem out of their control.

I wish you all the best on your current journey; whatever it may be.

Happy Trails,

Jane

Detour

Slow down and enjoy life. It's not only the scenery you miss by going fast – you also miss the sense of where you are going and why.

Eddie Cantor

Detour #1 – A Positively Devastating Road

I look at the world through rose-colored glasses, or so I'm told. I see the glass 1/2 full, look on the bright side, and try to see the good in people and bad situations. Other less optimistic types see me and my sanguine cohorts as meek, naive, clueless, unrealistic, etc. I'm here to tell you it takes a lot of work to be this way. It's not a gift or a "Barbie" trait. Nor is it a lack of experience or a dream-world existence. It's a conscious choice; one that takes knowledge, experience and skill. Feeling a spiritual or harmonious connection to life or the universe certainly helps, but it is groundedness and commitment that really keep it going.

I figure that keeping one's hopes up doesn't spark disappointment; it makes the way more pleasant. If disappointment happens, then you deal with it; if not-you've wasted no time on negative or unproductive energy. So with that said, here is my story.

After a stress filled summer of school, working over-time, not getting much exercise, I felt worn out. I thought I was out of shape and grouchy from the school/work combo. But then I felt different.

Detour

My heart began to beat harder and breathing wasn't so easy. Normal chores were becoming difficult, and my friends were saying I was a weird color. *A weird color?* Probably a decent reason to go to the doctor, not that heart palpitations and breathing issues weren't, but oh well..., sometimes I need other people to tell me what to do. So off I went, and guess what? My doctor said I was a weird color too, pale and anemic looking. So she did blood work, and 3 days later told me to come to the hospital right away as my blood was a mess and I needed a transfusion immediately. I had just worked a 10 hour day and then visited my elderly next-door neighbor and done my chores, and she's telling me immediately!

Turns out she suspected acute leukemia.

Turns out she was right.

And so I began a long journey into a whole new world that began with a diagnosis that was positively devastating. Long story short–I was admitted that night, in Reno, spent one night in the hospital receiving the blood and blessings of my dear friend Beth. Two days later I began the induction part of a very long treatment for acute lymphoblastic leukemia, or "ALL".

Detour

From an essay written early on in my treatment

How can one go from working a ten hour day, coming home and caring for an elderly neighbor, and feeding animals to being admitted into a hospital and receiving not only 2 units of blood, but a life-threatening diagnosis? On August 13, 2007, I went from living a hectic life of full-time work and part-time school to becoming a leukemia patient. I went from caring for neighbors and animals to planning a trip to a hospital 200 miles away where I would spend the next 28 days. I was told things like "You'll be going through your very own Vietnam War" and "the treatment is very intensive. Prepare yourself." I was scared, shocked, and anxious. My mind raced as I began to feel myself shrinking, as if everything in the room was getting bigger and I was fading into the background. The doctor was talking quickly and inundating me with information.

And then time stopped.

I could hear what was being said, but I could not respond. I felt as if I was being drained of the ability to process or react. My vessel – the part of me where my soul resides – was being emptied.

At times like this I would turn to God for guidance and protection, but that was in a "perfect world," one that I felt was slowly being taken away. "I should go within and find peace," I would tell myself, but I felt blank. I could summon no thoughts, good or bad. There was no blame, no "why me?" no anger; there was nothing. Time momentarily stood still and then continued in slow motion. I went from doing 3 things at once, going 90 miles an hour, to listening to doctors explain that, for the next year, I would be concentrating on only one thing - becoming healthy again.

Forget work. School was no longer a priority. My new "job" was to stay alive and that would take some strength and inner courage. But for all my keeping up on spiritual practice and being what I call "prayed up", I felt vacant, hollow and void of all I knew.

Stress – it's a crazy thing. Your mind takes over providing your body and soul some time to adjust. With me it was the feeling of shrinking. Becoming so small that I didn't have to speak. I could hear just fine, and I understood the gravity of the situation, but I did not want to speak. It took too much effort. I needed to process.

Looking back, I realize how everything just sort of happened. There were no questions of "how long will she live?" or "what if we do nothing?" The solutions fell remarkably into place, and I was more than willing to allow that. Despite the feeling of shrinking away, I truly felt guided and protected. My family, of course, wanted everything that could possibly be done to be done, but in retrospect, this came from a fear of death. We did little, if any, real discussion about it. I had the direct impression that with 90% blast cells in my blood (meaning 10% doing their job), time was of the essence.

When told I was suspected of having leukemia, I did not know what a "blast cell" was. Of course I'd heard of leukemia, even knew a guy in high school who died from it. We went to the hospital in Reno, where my husband, David, and I were walking in the 3rd floor hallway. He was explaining that my room was on the 3rd floor.

I stopped in my tracks and asked him if leukemia was cancer. He said he thought so, but he wasn't sure. "I'm pretty sure we are going to know more about leukemia than we ever planned."

The 3rd floor was where I visited friends who had cancer, some who had died there. I stopped and didn't want to go. David suggested I go ahead and get the blood I needed and we'd go from there. My sister Kate and friend Linda came to the hospital shortly after we arrived. I asked the oncology nurse about blast cells, as that was what was determining my diagnosis. I asked her if there were any other diseases or conditions that showed them in blood tests.

She said no.

Detour

From the first night in the hospital in Reno, when I was getting an IV for a blood transfusion, I realized that keeping a certain attitude would become a necessary way of life. The nurse couldn't find a decent vein; a problem that escalated as time went on. My veins became uncooperative and seemed to shrink much the same way my body felt when I was hearing the news of my diagnosis. She became a bit angered and started complaining about her horrible day. I'm lying there thinking, ok I just got a cancer diagnosis, and *you're* having a bad day???? Her lack of enthusiasm grated on my already fragile nerves. Thank God she finally called someone else; a wonderful, compassionate, smiling EMT from the Emergency Room who had no problem inserting the IV into my arm. I KNEW that was the care I wanted. So I put it out there, right then. One of my initial calls was to my friend Beth, who also happens to be a spiritual practitioner and is great with prayer. She showed up, sat quietly in the corner of my room, eyes closed in a meditative/prayerful state. Beth "held consciousness" meaning she went deep inside herself affirming that all really was ok, while all the crazy stuff was going on. While the nurse was telling me all the possible side effects and reactions to receiving blood, Beth looked at me, one eyebrow raised and a

Detour

sarcastic smirk on her face with her "not necessarily so" look, which always comforts me and humors me at the same time.

The blood had to be irradiated and processed and whatever, so it took awhile. It was getting very late and I hadn't received any blood yet. Everyone but Kate and Beth left and I tried to get them to go. I knew Beth had to get up early.

Her response is forever engrained in my memory. "I'm not going anywhere until I bless that damn blood."

This set precedence for me and my treatment. From this point on, any thing that went into my body – be it blood, platelets, chemo – was blessed along with the people who donated it, provided it, and administered it. Later, Beth gifted me a photograph of Nitro, her pet therapy dog and my friend, so that in her absence I would have a reminder of this. Nitro became my new "blesser".

After receiving my diagnosis the oncologist told me things like "Be prepared to enter your own Vietnam War" and "your only job for the next year will be to get healthy again." Vietnam? A whole Year? Truthfully I had never had the desire to go to Vietnam and at the time, I really liked my job. It was pretty overwhelming, but, true to my rose colored glasses, I took one step at a time and tried to remain positive.

Be careful what you wish for. Prior to learning I had leukemia, I was hoping to lose at least 10 pounds, have some time off, try a new haircut – maybe even really short…. You get my point. It was strange how these wishes manifested. Also in the year prior to illness I had been looking into a lot of cultures and spiritual practices. In truth, they came to me and I embraced them, eating up the information and digesting their meanings. I attended my first Passover dinner, a Ramadan celebration, built a drum and participated in ceremony related to that, went to a sweat lodge – it was all very enlightening. So when friends offered up prayers for me, I knew they would come in many different ways. Some would be the standard Christian 'ask God to protect me' while others put my name in prayer walls. Friends put my name on prayer request lists at numerous places of worship and spoke my name at Native American ceremonies. The variety was amazing and yet it all centered on offering to help.

Human nature is like that. People need something to "do" in a crisis. Prayer was something most of my friends were comfortable with and I was willing to accept. The odd thing was I didn't pray for myself. I had a peace about me that all would be fine, but my only prayers came in blessings and gratitude of others. I relaxed in the comfort of others' prayers, realizing it was one less thing to ponder. I found myself giving in to the idea that allowing myself to receive help from others was okay.

I was never one to ask for help; more of a "let me do it" type of person. I reveled in reaching out to others and lending a hand. I put my needs second to the needs of others and felt that was okay. I took giving seriously and thought of it as a spiritual practice. I still do, but in order to give, someone must receive. That realization hit home hard.

My indispensableness became dispensable in one phone call. I found out the world could still go on without my help and it took a cancer diagnosis to truly realize this.

With all the new information to process and so many things to think about, my mind shut off. I became void of emotions, unable to react. I felt no joy, no fear; I felt empty. In my deep subconscious I knew I was being guided, guarded, and protected, but the prayers would not come forth. At this moment, I realized the importance of receiving. As word of my illness got out, people began to pray for me. All different people, all different prayers. Friends and family reached out in any way possible, giving up a part of their lives to make mine more comfortable. Being on the receiving end was unusual, but for me it became vital. In the days that followed, I took up residence at UC Medical Center in San Francisco where I offered no resistance to the procedures and treatments that followed. Many were unpleasant, to say the least, but I thanked each person, knowing that what they offered was what I needed to stay alive. Gratitude became my prayer.

As days passed, it occurred to me how everything seemed to flow. Nothing seemed chaotic or overly disruptive. I could feel my vessel begin to fill. Knowing I was being held in prayer and in others' hearts and being grateful for this created a harmony within this challenge. I felt a certain peace and knew everything was going to be okay. Each infusion and procedure, while unpleasant, was temporary, and, when complete, it meant one more goal was met. Time continued to pass slowly as I understood I was learning mindfulness. Taking each moment and experiencing it without judgment or blame created a quiet place in my mind. This became a link to my vessel, that place where I felt a connection with Spirit. As my soul grew, I realized the emptiness was being replaced with love and gratitude, with forgiveness and surrender. In surrendering I was not giving up; I was accepting my circumstances and allowing the thoughts and prayers of others to fill my spirit. Through this experience, I learned that, when faced with my ultimate challenge, feeling nothing was simply the process of emptying my vessel. This was necessary to allow others to fill it with the love and faith I needed, when I could not muster it up myself. Others filling it led to instant gratitude which jump-started a chain of events leading to my healing.

There are times when we all feel spiritually challenged, overwhelmed to the point where our mind plays tricks on us and we feel unable to connect. With faith as a back-up and gratitude as a catalyst, the spiritual void in me was not only filled, but my excess overflowed into the lives of others. This overflow became apparent when my brother-in-law thanked me for experiencing this challenge, stating how he noticed the positive effect it was having on others' abilities to appreciate, simplify, and love. This experience had a similar effect on me as I still continue to use gratitude as my daily spiritual practice and graciously accept the offerings of love, prayer, and kindness. How can one go through a life-altering event without

Detour

disrupting the harmony and balance within? Truthfully, I found it very difficult, but for me, the healing began with gratitude and grew into mindfulness. I literally lived for the moment, taking each moment and accepting it as it was, embracing it even. I looked for reasons to be grateful and let go enough to allow others the gift of giving. Spirit is always present. Receiving is God's way of revealing that we truly are never alone.

8/15/2007 – A very long day. Driving to San Francisco and into the unknown. Scary – unforgiving good fun! Keep it light, it's a bit hard.

I like Dr. Martin.

More blood work.

I've lost more weight.

I'm doubting error.

Dr. Martin confirms "you have acute leukemia."

What kind?

More tests.

When?

10 minutes. A bone marrow biopsy.

We'll take bone marrow, a piece of bone from near your hip.

Detour

It wasn't bad. Demerol and adivan are my friends. So are Dr. Martin and Jabrila – and Sheila. Terra gives us good info, takes me to my room for the next month, then we wait. The kind of leukemia determines the treatment.

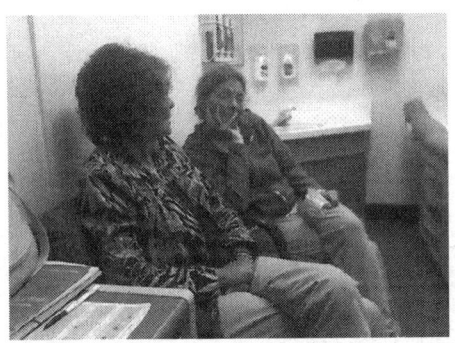

Me with my sister Kate waiting to see Dr. Martin

Acute Lymphoblastic Leukemia (ALL) comes in a mixed package. To determine the type of ALL, a bone marrow biopsy is performed. I had my first shortly after my official diagnosis at UCSF, two days after learning I was sick. I went into an examination room with a wonderful nurse named Sheila. Having just learned that my diagnosis was real and that I did have leukemia, and that leukemia was blood cancer, I sat down on the table and burst into tears. She was so kind and compassionate. I will never forget her. She sat next to me and put her arm around me and let me cry and then offered to get my husband. He came in, let me cry some more, and then left when the "big needle" came out. My twin sister took his place during the first of many intimidating procedures

I was given some Demerol and lay on the table on my stomach. Jabrila sat on a stool by my head, and I told her to talk to me, about anything. I just wanted her to keep talking and keep my mind off the procedure. She held my hand; her voice was calm and comforting as we started talking about her family and my job working with children. As the Demerol took effect I felt kind of floaty and good, and thought, "I feel stoned; and it's ok". Dr Martin gave me a local anesthesia and a few minutes later inserted a huge needle between my hip-bone and spine obtaining a "chunk" of bone marrow out of my pelvis. Sheila explained the procedure prior to its occurrence, so Dr. Martin was free to join our conversation. I bless him to this day for engaging me in the antics of his two year-old twins. Jabrila continued to hold my hand while Dr Martin jarred the inside of my pelvic bone, extracting the much-needed specimen. I gripped her tightly and squeezed my eyes shut and when it was over, I asked to see the sample. I was surprised how it looked just like the inside of a dog bone.

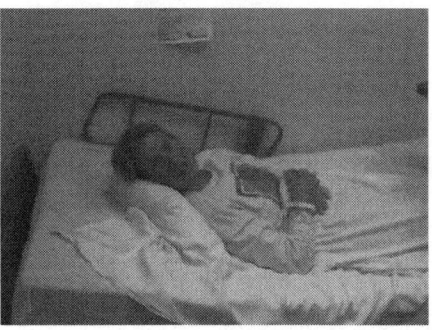

Shortly after my first bone marrow biopsy

Not long after the biopsy Nurse Terra explained blast cells as lazy teenagers that won't get out of your house. They just lie around and take up space so the other cells, the healthy ones, can't do their job. That night I dreamed about teenagers sitting around on a brown and orange plaid couch in the basement of my house, getting high and watching TV. I kept trying to get them to leave, but they ignored me.

This brought up a bit of a dilemma for me. I wanted them out, but the pacifist in me couldn't think of killing them even though they were killing me. Cancer diagnosis, treatments, meds – it all does funny things to your mind. I ended up wishing them into the ether where they could do no harm, but still be lazy teenagers. This is when

Detour

I realized I wasn't "battling" this disease. I wanted only positive energy around me and couldn't buy into the "cancer sucks" attitude. I'm not saying I thought it didn't. I just took a different approach to my own healing.

I was then wheeled across the street to the actual hospital and was admitted that day to 11 Long, my new home for the next month. My consultation appointment turned into the beginning of a long journey. As Terra pushed me across the street, she hesitated for a moment at the entrance and said, "Take a deep breath of fresh air. You won't have another one for a month." This is when real fear set in. As I breathed, I blessed the fresh air as if that one breath would strengthen me and remain in my lungs the entire stay.

11 Long is a wing of the hospital that serves hematology, oncology, and bone marrow transplant. It is actually 2 hallways with 3 patient rooms on the far end and the neuro ICU waiting room at the end where you get off the elevators (Neuro ICU was down a separate hallway in the attached Moffitt Hospital). In the very middle is a very busy nurse's station. There are also small offices and storage rooms. On the far end in the corners are family rooms. These are places patients can go to get out of their rooms and also to visit with family

Detour

and friends. They are larger and much more welcoming than a hospital room. They are a blessing on this floor, as most people stay a minimum of 3 or 4 days. One faces a hillside with Eucalyptus trees and had large couches, a game table, TV, videos, a computer and a bathroom with a shower for family members to use. It's big and a bit dark. The other room is all windows overlooking the Golden Gate Bridge, DeYoung museum, the SF bay, Kezar stadium, Golden Gate Park, etc. To the east you can see to the Trans-America Pyramid and to the north is an amazing scene where the bay meets the ocean under the bridge, back-dropped by the North Bay hills. It's a breathtakingly beautiful view. We were sufficiently blown away at this 5 star view; very impressive. Being unable to leave the floor for the next 28 days, I was happy to see that a place like this existed.

8/15/2007

I sleep, but awaken early. David gets
up to crawl part way in bed with me. It breaks my
heart to see him like this.
My sisters don't
fall apart in front of me.

Detour

I did a lot of writing in the hospital; journaling, poetry and things that popped into my mind in the middle of the night. It became a medium of reflection and processing. It was also a means of communication. David set-up an email listing called "Jane's' Leukemia Support Team," so that in order to write my family and friends all at once, I only had to write one letter. This was how he initially let people know about my diagnosis and kept them in touch.

Email from David: 8/17/2007

Please forgive me if I have left someone off this list, I am more concerned at this time about getting this news out and will add others as needed later. If you notice someone missing from this list, which will continue to grow, please pass this on and then please pass their email address on to me to include onto the list...

To all who are concerned and anxious about getting news about Jane, here is what we know so far...

Friday, August 10 Jane had a blood panel done because she had been experiencing shortness of breath. The results came back and it was about 90% that is was Acute Leukemia. After a subsequent test the original diagnosis was confirmed.

Detour

After a short stay in Renown in Reno, she was sent to the University of California at San Francisco for further tests. She had a bone marrow biopsy on Wednesday which determines the exact type of Leukemia. That brings us to today...Thursday about 4p, when the result came in that the type of Leukemia was identified as ALL or Acute Lymphocytic (or Lymphoblastic) Leukemia. We now know the immediate treatment will be a minimum of 5 weeks in UCSF with off and on chemo treatments. Further treatment is required but rather than go into detail, just know the chances of a 'cure' is historically about 90% without any further complications.

The next procedure is a spinal tap to see if the Leukemia has progressed into the spinal area. The results of this test will further define the treatment procedure and chemo chemistry. We should know the results of this test in several days. In about two weeks the results of the bone marrow test will show whether a bone marrow transplant is necessary. If necessary this usually comes from a close family member to ensure a cell match.

This all sounds pretty serious and frankly, it is. Jane will ultimately be in a weakened state but even then will still need support from all of you. She knows you all love her and are thinking of her at this time, but she is still going through some physically and psychologically stressful procedures, so we are not recommending calling or visiting her. If you feel you must call please wait 4 or 5 more days.

Please call her sister Kate prior to visiting. If you have an opportunity to visit, here are the "rules." Be aware that Jane now has a weakened immune system and visitors must not bring gifts, flowers, food and be very careful to disinfect their hands and wear a mask. If any coughing or sniffling is present or if you have been around anyone sick - please do not visit. Do not visit if you are experiencing any health issues. Jane's biggest threat of complications actually comes from infections introduced from the outside.

If things go well, Jane should be back in Reno sometime within 6 weeks.

Email is always welcome and Jane will try to check it as often as possible. Laughter and prayers are both healing, send both.

More information to follow,

David Wirth

Writing and receiving emails from others grew into somewhat of a spiritual practice for me. I wanted only to hear positive things and express positive things, so I wrote about the amazing things I was learning, the wonderful people I was meeting, and how the therapies were working. This compelled me to keep looking for the good and share the experience with others. However, I had days where my rose colored glasses remained, but I seemed to have misplaced them.

*8/16/2007 - The longest day! We wait; we take walks in and around the hallway. I'm so tired, but more blood helps. I wish I knew how I felt, but I don't. My emotions are bubbling around like the white water in a rapid. The only thing I understand is **trust**. I turn this over to others – higher powers – they come in all shapes and sizes.*

This is the day I started 8707, The Linker Protocol-the treatment that would hopefully get me into remission; the beginning of a very long journey towards "the cure." Until now I knew nothing about chemotherapy, how it was administered, what it looked like, or what it would feel like. It all began with getting a picc line. A really nice man came in, raised my bed higher than I could have imagined it would go, and draped me for surgery. It was all very sterile and I remember lots of little containers holding a variety of implements. He gave me a local anesthesia in my upper left arm and inserted a small tube that went up my vein all the way to the vena cava near the heart. I could see none of this because of the draping, but he explained it. Chemo is so toxic it can't go directly into your vein; it must meet up where there is a lot of blood flow. This was my understanding.

The procedure lasted about 45 minutes and was uncomfortable, but not painful. I felt a lot of pressure and, as requested by the picc line nurse, I took a lot of deep breaths. There were two ports poking out from my arm when he was finished. One was for chemo use only; the other for IV fluids, blood transfusions, and drawing blood. This was the bonus, as it meant no more poking in my arm trying to find a vein for blood draws. Afterwards there were x-rays to make sure the placement was right and then I was hooked up to the IV pole that had already become my permanent tether. Later that night the chemo arrived in a bag that was hung on the IV pole and hooked up to the port in my arm. It was a dark reddish color and one of the nurses referred to it as angel blood. I was so nervous I couldn't even think of a comeback. I pictured myself throwing up the moment it hit my veins. There were checks and cross checks by 2 nurses making sure what I was getting was the right drug, dose, and that I was indeed Jane Wirth born 7/20..., medical record number 48483...

By the end of the first week I had my medical record number memorized. As became our tradition with the first blood transfusion, we silently blessed the chemo for its healing properties, with Nitro faithfully looking on from his framed portrait. I watched it go through the tube and into my vein, officially starting my first of many chemo treatments. *The thin red line that looks so deceivingly like the life saving liquid. It too saves, but by taking away, not giving.*

The preceding procedures seemed endless; EKG's, chest x-rays, blood tests, pre meds all to make sure everything was ok and that my body would handle the toxic fluid. Once the chemo started, a nurse was in checking my vitals every 10 minutes or so. I think the treatment lasted 4 hours or so, but I don't really remember. I do remember being nervous about side effects and thinking my hair would fall out any second. I was given a lot of anti-nausea medicine during and after the treatment, and it worked, for the most, part pretty well.

Detour

8/17/2007 – Wondering, worrying, but I feel

very good! Great sign. My counts begin to drop

as they should, but I feel good. I get a shower, a walk,

and lots of small talk. Around 4pm I will receive

a lumbar puncture – oh crap! Kate doesn't understand

until she hears "spinal tap." I'd been downstairs for

an echocardiogram, but maybe that was yesterday.

I know for now I feel pretty good. My heart breaks

for others and there are only certain very strong

moments that I can talk with friends. I break down easily.

I take things one day at a time, no - one hour at a time.

When I feel good and all appears well, I bless that moment.

The yucky ones go by pretty fast.

I can't see the forest for the trees. It's too hard.

Right now I'm blessing the branches.

One often hears that it takes a special type of person to be a nurse, especially in a cancer ward; I found this to be amazingly true.

Detour

Never have I met and interacted with such kind and knowledgeable people. There I was, thrust into this seemingly impossible situation, asked to trust strangers with my life. The nurses at 11 Long made this so easy. I instantly felt assured and comforted by their care. Kari, my very first nurse at UCSF, treated me with compassion and respect. No one patronized or judged. I felt nothing but sincere concern, which was exactly what I needed. Procedures were explained honestly and openly. All questions were addressed, and believe me there were questions! It really made the beginning easier knowing I'd have the support of kind and caring people. I even befriended the housekeeping staff and the people who brought in meals. They treated me like family.

I was disappointed to learn that I'd not see Dr. Martin again for quite awhile, but soon got into the routine of the visiting "team." The team consisted of an oncologist, a fellow, a pharmacist, and a hospitalist. It was intimidating at first, but we all warmed up to each other daily. Again thank God for my sisters and husband who asked the right questions and got the doctors to explain things in layman's terms. My sister Kate was fastidious about writing everything down and keeping track of each treatment and procedure.

Detour

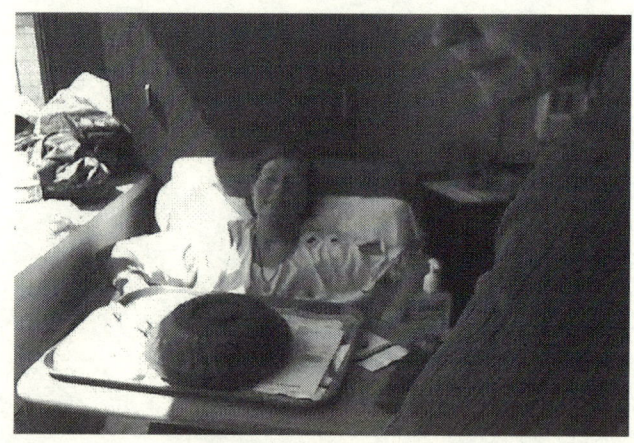

8/18/2007 – Not feeling too well today. Bad headache.

I think from the spinal tap; we renamed it lumbar acupuncture.

When they took the spinal fluid out some chemo

was put in. I think it caused some pressure.

Couldn't eat much, walked a bit. Mom came up

for a nice/short visit. Everyone is doing their falling

apart away from me. I appreciate it. There are

only so many times a day I can cry without it hurting

so much. I love the support and happily open myself

to everyone's prayers. I know my basic spiritual

beliefs are intact and always available; they're just a bit fuzzy.

Detour

Thank you Kate for keeping me alive and semi-sane

Thank you David for support that goes above and beyond

Thank you Jabrila for knowing when to be there

Thank you Tom – the baldness is a kind gift

8/19/2007 – No chemo last night. My heart didn't want to
cooperate. It wouldn't beat hard enough, 40 bpm
was it. Not enough to safely take the drug.
EJ, my nurse and the doctor thought it was because
of all the other drugs I get first. So its 7am and
I'm still waiting for a doctor's ok to give me the "Angel Blood"
or some other name they call chemo.
Today's affirmation: My heart is strong and works as a team
with the rest of my body leading the way to curative restoration.

I would get anxious when things did not go as planned. This was all so new to me and I thought if I veered off schedule, it would screw up the treatment. I later learned there is quite a bit of flexibility because everyone has a different reaction to treatment and that is definitely considered.

Detour

8/19/2007 – A surprise when mouth sores actually appeared. Food tastes strange now and sometimes it hurts to eat. My crotch has a sore and some very kind GYN ladies "ruptured" it. Oh what fun... It's actually 12:30am on the 21st, but I can't sleep. I think I slept through the 19th. It's a blur. Nancy came to see me and I liked that. I can be so honest with her. All in all Vietnam is going according to plan.

The anti-everything drugs worked pretty well for me. I felt more like I was coming down with the flu than actually having it. My energy level pretty much plummeted and I started getting really bad headaches, but I was encouraged to get up each and every day. So I walked the hallways, sometimes for awhile, sometimes for a couple of minutes and each step was a sign my body could still move and function, despite what my mind sometimes told it.

11 LONG

White hallways and floors
Beeping sounds
Busy nurses
Families gathered
Tears and fears
Loss and pain
11 Long
The floor of transitions
Always changing
It's no fun but there is laughter
It's traumatic but there is spirit
Your body is weak but you are strong
Illness is there
Healing is happening
Long days
    Long nights
        Long thoughts
            Long fears
                Long doctors
                    Long nurses
                        Long cleaning people
                          Long healing
                            Long hopes

Jabrila Via – 2007

Detour

Living at 11 Long was like going to a country I've never visited, with very friendly natives, but a stark sterile environment. I noticed immediately that the hallways served as a walking path for the patients. Once hooked up to my new "BFF", an I.V. pole that I would be tethered to for my entire stay, I ventured out. My sisters and David were there too. We explored the first of *many* laps around the hallways of 11 Long

Detour

8/23/2007 - I'm finally doing a cognitive task by writing to all of you wonderful friends who are filling me with love and light and support. It means a lot to know that I can count on your strength and support when mine seems muddled. So – it's been a trip! Not exactly the vacation in SF I was looking for but……. Right now, I think I've been here for 8 days. It all happened so fast and in a way I'm thankful for the lack of having to make major decisions. Thank God for my family!!!!! It's as if my whole world stopped in an instant, and now it is going in slow motion. As most of you know this is a complete 180 for me, but slow is my new mode. The treatment process is going well. I'll be here for at least a couple more weeks while they get the disease into remission. After that I will go home and rest and then begin again, this time to wipe it out completely. Days are long, but I am able to get up and around almost daily. The floor where I am staying is a big circle and I walk laps daily. I hear 12 laps is a mile! I'm not quite there. Like I said everything is in slow motion. The people in charge of my care are amazing!!!!!! Wonderful human beings filled with love and education and humor and compassion. They love to educate us too. So all in all – all is well. Thank you for your kindness, prayers, and love. It means everything to me. Until next time, know I love you all and feel blessed by each of you. Jane

For the most part I only wrote when I was feeling that way. Luckily, that was most of the time. Sometimes one must make the best out of a sketchy situation; this was one of those times. If I was going to be occupied under the premise of getting healthy for a whole year, I figured I'd better make it constructive. Sometimes I would wake up in the middle of the night, or not sleep at all: *"I spend my nights wondering while I drift in and out of dreams. My body so weary, yet my mind constantly changing cars on a bullet train"*. I'd write random things that usually cracked me up the next day: *"I wonder what will happen to the bugs that live in my eyelashes when my hair falls out. Will they live forever on a fallen follicle or perhaps find a new host; one with hair"*.

At this point I still did not know if I needed a bone marrow transplant, I didn't realize the extent of my hospital stays, had no clue about insurance or how long I would be away from work. The doctor said one year, but I assumed that meant a couple months of intense treatment followed by a less intense able-to-go-back-to-work kind of remedy. Yeah, right. The protocol I was on suggested a 90% cure rate for ALL and an 80% cure rate if a transplant was necessary.

First, there is the Induction… which means many intensive chemotherapy treatments, along with other medication to zap your body into remission. This series proposes the following schedule: 28 days in the hospital, 10 days home, 21 days in the hospital, 10 days home, 4 days in the hospital 7 days home 4 days in the hospital. It was now August so I was looking at being in treatment until Thanksgiving or so. Well, unfortunately, I didn't get the picture quite right. As it turns out, the series once completed is repeated! And there are 2 more 4-day stays tacked onto the end! And if all went as planned, I'd now be done in February – again, yeah right.

What can I say – shit happens.

8/25/2007 - ALL results from an acquired genetic injury to the DNA of a single cell in the bone marrow. This was an explanation in one of the many pamphlets I was handed at the beginning of this journey; one that sort of made sense as no other explanation is really ever given. I wonder when this happened. Was it recently or building up over a lifetime? Did I feel it?

Detour

Did I somehow sense it – "oh genetic injury, I hope it heals" as if I twisted my ankle and hoped I hadn't sprained it. The cellular level is pretty amazing.

If something so small can cause all this, then it is truly a wonder – a miracle—

that so many people are intact.

Crazy things are coming around. I've been delving into religious/spiritual ceremonies and rituals this past year.

Now I find people are praying for me from a huge variety of sects and teachings.

I gave some of my sick time away, now I'm using it for myself.

I gave my hair away, now I'm losing it. It's all so strange.

Was this path planned, created or coincidental?

It's a lot to process.

In my healthy world of active happy friends and family, the diagnosis of leukemia came as more than just a shock. It rocked the worlds of many who began to question their own mortality and rethink their daily lives. Many people told me that my illness changed their life, and for the better.

Detour

But in the halls of 11 Long it was a totally different world. I had the "good" kind of leukemia. I was one of the "healthy" ones. For all the devastation this disease caused me and my family, I was considered lucky by many.

11 Long became a second home to me with the staff becoming like family. For all the insecurity and fear that comes with a lengthy hospital stay, it was okay being at 11 Long. I felt safe and cared for. For the first few days I talked only to nurses, doctors, family, etc.

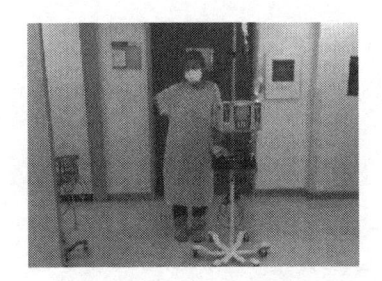

My sisters were becoming quite familiar with the lay of the land and had already met numerous patients. I was reluctant to talk to anyone at first, being so wrapped up in my own world, but I eventually settled into conversations with others. I did not know how to talk to people about their illness. Dare I ask why they were there? I learned a new "lingo," one that offered an entrance into subtle conversation. I easily used words like diagnosis and picc line. Biopsy and transplant became part of everyday conversation along with length of stay. "How long are you here for?", as if we were imprisoned by a crime committed against us. Chemo, neutropenic, blood counts, rolled off our tongues as if we were doctors. We were all getting our master's degrees in blood cancer through experience.

That was the advantage of going through treatment in-hospital. I never felt isolated. I could converse with nurses who gave awesome, clear explanations, but the other patients, the ones going through treatment, were the ones who understood and offered support, most often without even knowing it.

One of my first rallyers was Ron. He was getting ready for a transplant and taking it all seriously. He'd cruise the halls at quite a clip and he knew practically everyone. He quickly became my role model.

My second stay was near Halloween. Ron's partner decorated his IV pole with barbed wire and bats – very becoming. It started a movement as I noticed more and more Halloween decorations appearing throughout the halls and rooms, and on the poles. Ron always had something good to say. And he knew a lot about planes. We watched Fleet Week together from the solarium where he

Detour

educated me on a variety of aeronautical facts. It was during this time that I met Dave also. His wife Lorraine and I had become friends through walking the halls, but Dave was often in his room. It was good to finally see who went with Lorraine. He appeared in a wheelchair and dozed off and on while we watched the air show right outside the window of the solarium.

Dave also knew a lot about planes and shared some of his knowledge despite his groggy state. The Blue Angels appeared and disappeared for days prior to this, practicing and performing. We would check the schedule of events to see when they would be airborne so we could watch. My sister Kate even came a day early to see the final show. By the end of Fleet Week, I felt I never needed to see another air show.

By the end of the year, the planes would still be there, but both Dave and Ron would be dead from a myriad of effects caused by such a crappy disease.

Detour

Cancer is not a private battle. From the second

you hear the words or even think you hear the words,

it gets involved with others, with God, with everything.

I am the only one who knows how I feel but I don't even

know that. It's all so surreal; not just the "this may cause death

thing,"

but what it takes to go through it all. And it is not done alone.

Everyone has someone and I am lucky to have many.

I am blessed by this, but also overwhelmed.

The effect this disease, my illness, has on others is difficult, hard,

heartbreaking.

I cry every time I think of my mom and what she must be going

through.

I'm trying not to break my spirit; I need it now more than ever,

but my heart is aching for others.

Detour

After about 2 weeks, we found out I did not have the funky chromosome that meant needing a bone marrow transplant! I was so relieved, only to find out I had another abnormality that the doctors didn't know how to address: my seventh chromosome.

It was missing an arm. Sounds strange I know, but under the circumstances it really upset me. What does that mean? How will it affect me? Because I didn't know the answers and the doctors didn't really have an answer either, David put on rose colored glasses with me, and we decided it meant that my treatment would be the most successful ever and a cure would be imminent. Why not? When faced with doubts, why not go for the extreme positive? How many times have we gone for the extreme negative – you know "worse case scenario"? No one pulls that rug out from under you, so why not the other way?

As of this writing I still don't know the actual medical effects of the above-mentioned missing limb, but truthfully it doesn't matter. My friend Linda thinks that Jabrila, my twin, probably took it in-utero and has two. Some people will say anything to evoke humor.

This one worked for me.

Detour

When I first entered the hospital, I had 90% Leukemia cells in my blood. That number had been reduced to 15% as of August 30th and is most likely lower by now as I have had more major chemo treatments.

Additionally, I've tested negative for the PH chromosome, which makes my prognosis even better! Yay!

First round of treatment should be completed by Sept. 12th. The goal is complete remission. Then home for about a week and back for round two which is a little more aggressive but oriented towards the cure. Subsequent treatments are yet to be determined.

This is the beginning of a long process so hearing from everyone and knowing they are thinking and praying for the cure is extremely helpful!

Detour

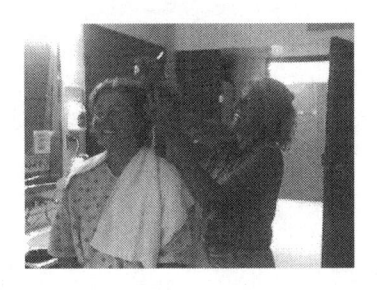

Taking Control –

My hair was going to leave, so I let my sisters play Barbie with it. When my hair began to obviously fall out, I asked Gabby, a nurse to shave my head. It was nice to be able to take control of something. During this time, my sisters and I amused ourselves by making up songs about my treatment. To the tune of the 12 days of Christmas:

5 types of chemo

4 lumbar punctures

3 bone marrow biopsies

2 fun sisters

And a haircut by an organic farmer

I think we were all getting "chemo brain."

On the lighter side, my sisters have stopped playing "Barbie" with my hair, which is starting to fall out, and now I look like Ken!

Detour

The first 28 days passed with a slowness that was wearing. I'd look at the clock and think "it's only 9:30?" and I'd wonder how I'd make it through the day, never mind the week. My half-crazed brain kept me quite entertained. I don't know if it was the cancer or the meds, but those first 28 days I hallucinated a lot! I knew what I was seeing wasn't real and I didn't feel particularly stoned, but the images were odd. Mostly sad, sometimes creepy, but I wasn't scared. Just amazed at what my brain was doing. Looking into the eucalyptus trees I saw monsters and pirate ships, lots of dark and unsettling creatures. There was a picture hanging in my room of two girls in a pasture with sheep and a house. Maybe water, I don't remember. It was very soothing, or supposed to be. Pastel colors, pastoral scene…but it saddened me. One girl was always sad. She had angel wings (in my head, not in the picture) but she was not a bright-coming-to-save-me type of angel. She carried despair on her wings. I tried to mentally change the scene, but each time I looked at it, the dismal angel couldn't seem to get her bright on. It was all very melancholy.

During this time I had a lot of crazy dreams. In one of the most remarkable ones, I was in a department store elevator going up. The door opened and I was in this amazing room. It was like the dining room section of the store, but the light was amazing. It was like pictures you see of Heaven – all cloudy and ethereal. There was a table all set with beautiful linens, and the silverware and plates were trimmed with brilliant diamonds and jewels. I am not usually a jewel-type person, but this was unbelievably beautiful. So beautiful I could feel it. It took my breath away and made me feel peaceful and wonderful.

It was so vivid, that when I woke up, I thought for sure I had died and seen heaven; which is odd because I don't believe in Heaven, at least not by the traditional definition.

My connection to "Spirit" or God began at an early age. Each Sunday my family went to church and we kids went to Sunday school. Mostly I remember singing pretty songs that made me feel good. However, I grew to know God through nature and the natural world. Church was fun, but my deep spiritual beliefs are best evoked while walking in the mountains or sitting by a lake. This is where I appreciate and feel God's presence the most. As for the afterlife, I am truly uncertain. I don't believe our time on earth is meant to send us to heaven or hell for all eternity, but tend to think of life as everlasting; a continuation on different planes after death. What those planes look like is where it gets muddled. I often thought about stuff like this.

Each day I would take some time to sit in the sunlight through the window, read so my mind could stay focused, or answer emails.

I walked daily, one or two laps at a time, far from the twelve that equaled a mile. My body was withering away. About 11:30 each morning, the kitchen began to cook something...not sure what, but the smell drifted up through the vent into my room and made me absolutely nauseated. My appetite was pretty non-existent anyway and that smell wafting through my nostrils left me feeling like I had the stomach flu. I'd usually try to leave at that time. If I was getting some sort of procedure or treatment, I'd have to just take it. The smell even affected my sister and niece.

I'd walk the halls and at the end was a waiting room for the Neuro ICU. I could see my reflection in the glass and noticed my ass disappeared. It was crazy; just gone! I kept wondering how I was going to sit down without an ass! Also my ankles. I was lying in bed one afternoon and my sister Annie was visiting. I showed her my ankles and legs. They looked so tiny. I was convinced I'd wither to nothing and eventually get lost in my own bed. It's odd to watch that happen to one's own body. I'd wanted to lose some weight for years, but this was ridiculous. Eating was not much of an option. I had some nutritional drinks sometimes, but even those were hard to gag down.

I'd quit coffee without even knowing it and suffered incredible headaches. They offered to mainline me with caffeine (seriously) but I opted for a pill that had a pain killer along with caffeine. It was amazing.

Dr. Patrick Gamp, a hospital internist, was my hero on many levels. He was my constant throughout all 130 + days I spent in the hospital, and he became a friend. He'd listen, not act like I was crazy, and try to solve my ever-multiplying dilemmas. Constipation has never struck me as life threatening, but I tell you what – after a few days my body reacted violently. One of the chemo drugs, vincristine, causes constipation by seizing up the bowels. They become sort of paralyzed and can't do their job. The problem is that you have to poop (everyone becomes creepily involved in your body functions) before you can have the next dose. The doctors and nurses like to keep the protocol pretty regular, so pooping becomes important.

Detour

Patrick took this very seriously and started me on laxatives. When one didn't work, he'd switch. I ended up taking this horrible syrupy shit called lactulose. I'd chase it down with cranapple juice or seven up. Drinking it would almost make me puke. I had it once, waited, then another dose. This went on for about a day and a half, and to add to the already compounding pressure, it gave me gas. My sister called my friend and neighbor Linda – a devout horsewoman – and said "Jane's colicking and we don't know what to do!" She recommended rubbing tar on my belly…I think I'll pass. So we walked and walked and bent and scrunched and tried to find relief from the most uncomfortable/painful bellyache I've ever experienced. Patrick walked in once and found me on my bed, backwards, on all fours in total misery trying to relieve the pressure and pain. He said "wow- sorry about all this... I did that to you". For some reason it made me laugh. This went on for awhile longer until finally – 6 doses into it, relief came…for days.

Then another dose of vincristine, and it started all over again… The next time the nurse gave me morphine. Ahhh. There's nothing like sleeping through the pain.

Detour

One morning a nurse, checking my picc line as they often do, noticed redness to the area around the line. She called in the head nurse who said it was becoming infected, so out it came. An internist came in and explained he would be pulling the line. He then cut the stitches holding the line in and asked me to take a deep breath. I did and as I slowly let out my breath, he slowly pulled out the line. I couldn't really feel it, but watched in amazement at its length, which was about 8 to 10 inches long. I was draped and unable to watch it go in, so seeing it come out was quite honestly, fascinating. And quick! The picc line nurse was unavailable so I had about half an hour of untethered freedom. I literally jumped out of bed and asked my sister Jabrila to walk the hallways with me. It felt so great to walk without dragging the IV pole. In the hallway I encountered a nurse, showing him I could turn in a circle. It was so exciting. He put his finger on the top of my head and I turned circles like a jewelry box ballerina. Jabrila was laughing and for that moment, I was having fun. It's funny how a simple act can induce such joy. I returned to my room to find the picc line nurse awaiting my arrival. He once again inserted another picc line, in my right arm this time, and I returned to my tethered state.

Detour

Laughter is the best medicine. I've heard that, but now I know it truly is! Making jokes to ease the tension is a family trait and we used it often. The first big release came a couple of weeks into treatment, late one night in my hospital room. Kate and I were playing cribbage, and I was winning. At first I thought – oh my God, she's letting me win because she feels sorry for me – and that creeped me out. My mind turned to thoughts of a conspiracy of kindness. I wanted, needed, people to not feel sorry for me. I wondered if everyone would start letting me win at cards and send fake greetings because they felt they should. And then she got a great hand and started winning. We were neck to neck coming down the home stretch and I got the crappiest hand ever. I looked up at her and sighed, "Oh, great, life has just dealt me another bad hand." She stared at me for about 2 seconds and then we started laughing so hard that we were rolling, crying, holding our sides. We couldn't even look at each other. This turned into a 10 minute exchange of bad cancer jokes. "I suppose you're going to start playing the cancer card" she finally said and I turned over the Ace of spades from the deck - the death card! That totally cracked us up. I told her if I died in my sleep, she'd regret beating me at cribbage. "Uh uh honey – that

Detour

would make me the champ." We continued making up inappropriate scenarios and became almost hysterical.

"Oh can I move to the front of the line? I have cancer."

"Oh, was I speeding Officer? I am so sorry, I'm late for my chemo treatment."

"I'm sorry this bill is late; I'm going through cancer treatment and..."

I realized it was okay to talk like that. I had cancer. I could make jokes about it. And it felt great! We stayed in that state for awhile, until Kate said we needed to be quieter, or they'd kick us out. Ok, I'm hooked up to an IV pole, in a bed on a hematology-oncology unit that NO ONE leaves, receiving toxic chemicals; you get the picture – so of course my retort was "they won't kick *me* out."

That being said, the days were definitely not all laughter and fun. For the most part it was zero energy, followed by waves of nausea, followed by mouth sores, indigestion, bone pain, no appetite, blood clots, spinal taps, bone marrow biopsies, etc. No bed of roses. What kept me going was knowing that each one of these was a temporary state. I was in treatment and there was an end to it. Far off maybe, but there was an end. Each horrible moment would eventually be eased and the next one might be better. I totally understood and embraced the "living for the moment" concept. A procedure may take 30 minutes, but it was followed by the relief of it being done. I learned to put my mind in a totally separate place from my body.

 The drugs also helped.

8/29/2007 - Hello from 11 Long (that's the name of the hospital unit I am on). All is going swimmingly (sometimes it feel more like drowning), but all in all things are progressing well. Thanks for all the cards and emails, it's so great to hear something daily. You are all so caring and thoughtful. Believe me it is helping! I had my second bone marrow biopsy this morning and tomorrow should bring results from that as well as the one 2 weeks ago. Basically it will show how well the treatment is progressing (and we all know that answer!) and will narrow down the type of A.L.L. even further. Tomorrow begins a new round of chemo and within 10 days or so that will be complete. My wonderful Kate is leaving today or tomorrow for a much-deserved break. Jabrila is here and will take over for a week. It's so nice to have such a supportive family. UCSF has such great people with such interesting backgrounds. It's been good getting to know them. I've met a few patients too and we all *cheer each other on. Thanks again for the moral and spiritual support. Its working wonders! I will update you again soon.*

Love, Jane

Prior to my diagnosis I was seeking holistic medical help for chronic sinus infections. I engaged the services of a wonderful acupuncturist who kept me off antibiotics for well over a year. I was sold on eastern medical philosophies and began eating more nutritious foods and stopped western meds almost entirely; even over-the-counter remedies for allergies and headaches. I knew the pressure points to use and could call Gary, my acupuncturist, whenever I felt the need for a treatment. Even he became concerned, though, at my lack of energy and breathlessness. He suggested blood work, stating that my blood was very deficient. The results would help him determine the best treatment. What a surprise to find out just how deficient my blood really was. And so I went from this lovely non-substance, natural healing, non-invasive life to entering chemical warfare.

In western medicine, when a drug doesn't work or it has a side effect, there's another one that will counter-act it and one more to fix the problems caused by the counteracting med. The process seems endless. This is carried out to keep the patient comfortable. I welcomed this comfort and succumbed to western medicine easily, as I saw no alternative at the moment. I'm sure, given time for researching holistic approaches or diet alternatives, I could have gained wonderful information and possibly a different type of treatment, but I was encouraged to be quick and aggressive in my treatment. Further, I chose a university medical center for my care and, while they offer a variety of awesome support, the treatment is chemical warfare. And the treatment worked. After the induction treatment (initial treatment to really blast the hell out of the blast cells) was complete and I went on maintenance, I went back to the acupuncturist. It's funny how the western med docs look at me suspiciously when I mention acupuncture, and Gary, my acupuncturist, rolls his eyes at the side effects caused by the chemo treatments.

Detour

Good Morning,

Jane has suggested that everyone who is wondering how they can help can donate blood. You can say it's for her, but the blood she actually receives is from the general blood bank.

Jane says that "each blood bag says 'volunteer donor' and she will know it's from you." She also says "it truly does save lives." Every transfusion has literally turned her pink again and raised her energy level. This is not a request for her personally, but for all who need blood and blood products. She feels donating blood is truly donating life and to anyone who is capable of doing so, we encourage you to donate. Thank you for considering such an awesome gift. David

Detour

9/12/2007 - What a difference a day makes

After a very challenging week, I am happy to report that my blood counts are up and I am going home on Friday! I will only be there a week, but it will be nice to breathe fresh air, have a change of scenery, be untethered from my IV pole and recover a bit in my own home. I probably won't send emails from home next week. I just will be appreciating being there. Kate and I un-decorated my room today and it looks so plain. Thanks again for all the lovely cards, pictures, and prayers. I think of you all often with love.

Next round is another 30 day gig here on 11 Long. The chemo will be more aggressive but headed towards the cure. Will let you know what's going on in the future. Until then, know I feel blessed by each and every one of you.

Your (temporarily) skinny and bald friend, Jane

Detour

After 28 days of fun and frolic at UCSF, I was finally released to "go home and rest" for 10 days. God knows you can't rest in a hospital. So off I went, with sister, Kate. I remember getting out of the wheelchair and standing for the first time, outside in the first fresh air I'd breathed in 28 days. It was wonderful and shocking all at the same time. The body weakens significantly with bed rest and chemotherapy. It became quickly apparent that I was not the same as when I went in! She pulled the car around and I gratefully got in. We drove through Golden Gate Park and I opened the window and stuck my nose out like a dog. It was as if I'd never seen a tree or a flower or breathed in fresh air before. I couldn't get enough. On the way home I stopped at a store as I wanted a Dr. Pepper or Coke or something to settle my stomach. Kate offered to go, but I wanted to get out and stretch. It felt like I was now living in a different body and different head. It was so strange how weak and spaced out I was. I did manage to get a drink and pay for it, but truthfully, it was really difficult. I felt like when I was younger and went into a store trying to pretend I wasn't stoned, or drunk, or whatever and working so hard at not "blowing it." The paranoia didn't accompany me because the fear of collapsing was so much stronger.

I think we stayed that night at my sister Annie's in Vacaville and continued home the next morning. It was SO unbelievably wonderful to be home and on my own couch. We were all so worried about doing something wrong, that we read all the paperwork, made all the necessary appointments, and made sure the house was clean and no one with germs would come around.

That being said – I was able to relax and enjoy my home.

For about 2 days.

That's when the chest pains began. I called the number at UCSF to talk with a nurse and he said it was probably acute indigestion due to the chemo and all the meds, but if it became worse or I got feverish to go to the E.R. I've never been to the E.R. as a patient and wasn't inclined to try it, but Monday morning about 4am, I couldn't stand the pain any more. Indigestion or not, I needed something. I woke David up and he drove me to the local hospital. He also called my friend Linda and my sister, Kate. Kate, of course, was there almost before we were. By the time I got to the admitting desk I was doubled over and throwing up. Luckily I got right in and they fixed me a GI cocktail. I had high hopes that this would work and I'd be on my way home.

No such luck. Never ask what else could go wrong.

Seriously, never!

One of the tests showed elevated heart enzymes so now I was to be admitted as a heart patient! My blood work also showed that I was again neutropenic, (low white count-high risk of infection) so I had to have a room to myself and be in "reverse isolation", meaning anyone coming into my room had to wear a crazy yellow outfit, like a scrub thing, with gloves and a mask. I spent the next couple of days going through a series of tests. That night, by order of Dr. Martin at UCSF, I had another bone marrow biopsy. Luckily my friend Linda had just arrived and was willing to talk to me during the procedure. As with Jabrila, I told her – "I don't care what you say, just talk to me. Keep me engaged until it's over." And she did. She was a little blown away at the size of the instrument and the violation of my pelvic bone. I felt little. The doctor gave me the memory drug, but I decided to see if it was for real and fought the urge to sleep through it. I did remember most of it. Mostly I remember Linda being there with me, holding my hand, with a look of confused concern on her face; as if she really could not believe any of this was happening. She was becoming aware of my new world.

The next day I had a heart test. Because I was way too weak to do a treadmill test, they chemically induced a rising heart rate. It was a crazy array of tests where I had an x-ray (sort of) of my heart, before and after this chemical heart-high. The technician was a friend of Linda's, which made the whole thing better. It was so hi-tech, it was creepy. At the end of the test I was waiting in a waiting room to be sure they didn't need anything else, and I got really cold. I mean bone-chilling, could not get warm, cold. As I sat there shaking, someone brought me heated blankets. By the time I got back to my room I was throwing up and had a fever of 104 degrees. Was it the test? They said no; I suspect my body was rejecting everything at this point, but who knows? Later, while still in Reno, the UCSF nurse said it was probably a neutropenic fever because, after all that, my blood counts plummeted. I spent the next 8 days in the hospital. Shortly after being admitted I noticed an aching in my right arm; the one with the picc-line in it. I thought it was from being on the gurney in the ER for so long, but no…another complication. For a couple of days I complained about it and the nurses gave me pain meds. Finally I called the head nurse at UCSF because I was so afraid my treatment was getting screwed up and the last thing I wanted was to start over. I was supposed to be back at UCSF and I was in the hospital in Reno. I told her about the pain in my arm and she told me to have them do an ultrasound immediately. I did and they actually listened. The picc line had caused a blood clot.

Again I remind you…NEVER ask "what else?" Not long before I found out the results, the minister of my church came to call. I really wasn't supposed to have many visitors, but ministers have a lot of clout in a hospital! She was there, across the room wearing the crazy yellow outfit, when the doc came in and told me about the clot. Now normally I would have completely freaked out with that news, but as he was telling me I noticed Reverend Liesa sitting calmly with her eyes closed. I knew she was praying for me. I could see it and feel it. My would-be-hysteria was replaced by calmness as he explained the upcoming procedures, blood tests to determine the amount of meds needed and then blood thinners, and it seemed okay. I, again, was given the gift of another aligning the universe in a way that lended to my good. At that moment it was just what I needed to ward off negativity and keep my attitude and heart lifted. And once again I was blessed with a moment of gratitude I will never forget.

Later that day the picc line was removed from my right arm. The nurse cut the stitches that held the line, and then pulled the line from my arm. No deep breaths, just cut and pull. I was then draped, given local anesthesia and a new line was inserted back in my left arm. The procedure was much the same as the last two.

Prior to my diagnosis, I was helping my next door neighbor and friend, Glenna. Glenna was a feisty 85 year old who suffered from COPD and never left her house. I did her shopping, took her to the doctor, helped her organize her medications, etc. She was in the same Reno hospital at the same time I was, on the same floor, just a few rooms away. She was in the ICU unit, so when she appeared in my room wearing the yellow protection outfit I was quite surprised. A nurse wheeled her in asking if it was okay for her to visit. Of course I agreed, as I hadn't seen her since my quick disappearance just over a month ago. I asked her how she managed to get out of her room and into mine. She replied, "I got in my chair and wheeled myself out the door. The nurse said I couldn't go so I told her 'just try to stop me.'" Glenna was a very determine, and at times intimidating, woman. I

64

was so happy to see her. I asked her how she liked my new haircut and she said it was beautiful. She was so pleasant and sweet, I would hardly guess how sick she really was. We talked about missing home and after just a few minutes a nurse came in and wheeled her off. She told me she loved me and I told her the same. It was the last time I saw her.

My quick emergency room visit lasted 8 days. In the beginning I felt so horrible that I realized death wouldn't really be a bad way out. I felt at peace with it. I wasn't suicidal or anything. I just felt okay with my own passing.

A couple of days later a report came on the news that Reno was getting a semi-pro baseball team. I thought about how fun it would be to go to opening day. I called my brother-in-law, an avid fan, and told him about. He too was really excited. Then it dawned on me. I was planning something for the future, something 7 months down the road. It was the first time since my diagnosis that I had a "normal" thought. If I went to opening day, it would be after this treatment was all over. What a concept…

I started feeling a lot better after 5 days, but because of the blood clot, they had to get my Coumadin levels right. During this time

Detour

I was "supplemented" with louvenex, another blood thinner given by injection. After 3 days of this crap, I asked if I could give myself the shot and go home. I was seriously thinking I was losing my mind! During this stay, it took all I had to remain in a positive state. I almost didn't pull it off. I became so depressed and wanted out SO badly.

It took most of Monday to release me from the hospital. The discharge nurse couldn't get in touch with the doctor from infectious diseases, who was the one determining my stay. In the meantime I learned how to give myself a stomach injection, and I then had to demonstrate. It was weird, but SO worth the reward of going home. Little did I know that I would become an expert at those little injections. Kate waited patiently with me, and finally around 4pm I was free! The air was so welcome, and again I rode home like a dog hanging my head out the window. I was so happy to be home I felt almost high.

9/25/07

Hello everyone – after a rather rough week I am happy to report I am comfortably and happily at my own home relaxing for 2 days! Home never felt so good! I'm feeling much stronger and actually feel great today. (Not that I'm signing up for a marathon or anything...) I return to SF on Thursday and will be there about a month. I never tire of telling you all how much I appreciate your love and support. I am blessed with an amazing network of people and I truly am grateful to each and every one of you. Know in your hearts that my healing is progressing perfectly and take time to thank yourselves for your part in it. I Love you all!! Jane

It's a little odd. In retrospect I realize that during my treatment, the hospital (UCSF) became like my home, and home became like a vacation, where I went to recover. Regardless, home was great. I went out back and visited the horses, and Kate walked with me around our circle driveway. Two times was all I could muster. I stayed home for about 2 days then had to return to UCSF for my next stay of 21 days. During those 2 days I had a few visitors, but mostly enjoyed the freedom of moving at my own pace without an IV pole attached. David continued to work so I had some alone time, which I relished! It was peaceful, pain-free, and other than being totally wiped out, wonderful.

Detour

The following Thursday I went back to 11 Long: my old/new home. I was greeted by Patrick who shook his head and said something like "wow Jane, we can't leave you anywhere!" We talked about the whole chest pain incident and he thought that maybe the clot had something to do with it. That maybe a part of it broke off and went to my heart. No way to really know, but I was grateful he cared.

On the way to SF, David had taken the scenic route. We drove up over Mt Rose and around the north shore of Lake Tahoe, so I could breath in the mountain air and drink in the beauty before being cloistered for another 3 weeks. David was very considerate like that; always doing the little extra things to make me happy. This whole thing was SO hard on him; I can't even imagine. It's one thing to have a disease attack your body and go through hell and back trying to get rid of it. But watching someone you love go through it–it's got to feel so helpless and …like I said, I can't imagine.

So off we went on as many back routes as we could. When we got to San Rafael, we stopped at Burger King for junk food. I figured my body had so many chemicals and crap going through it, what was a little more? Plus the protein of a hamburger sounded great. On the way down I was noticing a familiar ache in my arm, which increased throughout the day. As we pulled into the parking lot for burgers, I started sobbing and told David I thought my new picc line was clotting. Again, he remained calm and let me sob for a bit. It was a very quiet lunch. We checked in at the clinic and I told the nurse about the ache. She did all the preliminary blood work, ordered an ultrasound, and found yes, another clot. I now had to be on lovenox, the tummy shots, until Valentine's Day. Once again the line was pulled, with a deep breath out this time. Because picc lines were no longer an option, I was sent to a medieval torture dungeon (the IR Department). I was given adivan to relax me, but found it did nothing to alleviate the pain of getting a central line. After local anesthesia, the doctors stabbed me profusely in the neck inserting a line. At least that's what it felt like to me. The local helped with the initial cut, but the insertion was horrible. It was the first time I cried during a treatment. I watched the clock thinking to myself, this should only take five minutes. I can handle this. Just keep watching the clock. And so for the next couple of minutes I concentrated on the second hand and tried to think of nothing else. When it was over I was sent to a recovery room, and then wheeled back to my room. I felt like I had whiplash and a stab wound. This was no fun at all.

Detour

The good news: it didn't clot.

The bad news: I had to have it removed and reinserted another 3 times.

9/28/07 – Ultrasound in right arm, clot resolving but still blocking the vein. Left side, new clot at picc line – line will come out and be replaced with one near my collar bone – otherwise feeling great. – Later – replaced with central line on the left side of my neck. Very painful – left arm picc removed, chemo started around midnight –
Etoposide and Cytarbine. Lots of pre meds and pain meds tonight.

9/29/07 – Woke up at 6:30 throwing up. No fun. More meds, slept through the day and through all visitors.
Moved to room 1127, private and received 2 units of blood.
Chemo at Midnight.

So I experienced a whole new round of chemo this time – supposed to be the "aggressive type." I'm still wondering what that first round was… The friendly type?

Detour

My first dose caused me to wake up puking, so I got some meds and slept through my brother's visit. I started in a shared room and shortly was moved to a private one. It was quiet and cozy. My sister Jabrila came, and together we watched movies and walked the halls.

At this point, I felt like putting my rose-colored glasses aside. I stopped writing this book. Or so I thought.

Detour #2 - The journey continues; the road is bumpy, but begins to smooth

Back to my second round of treatment, back to 11 Long, back to my midnight scribblings and email history. Back to my detour.

10/1/2007

Happy 1st day of October. I got back to UCSF on Thursday with yet another blood clot in my arm. I now have a Frankenstein looking apparatus in my neck serving as a central line. Just in time for Halloween! Treatment began with nausea and puking, but thanks to the wonder drugs around here I mostly just slept through it. I get up and walk in the afternoon and that's good. My appetite is still fair, good even. Jabrila is here and must get bored watching me sleep. The chemo – 2 types – is for only 4 days, and then we wait for it to do its thing. Take me down and build me back up. Should take 2 to 3 weeks. Getting sleepy now but will write when I can. THANKS for the beautiful prayer flag. It's quite the conversation piece. And thanks for the continued love and good wishes. It means everything.

Xoxo Jane

Detour

10/1/07 Very groggy and sleepy. Ate breakfast and showered – not much energy. No nausea.

10/2/07 No energy, headachy, uncomfortable

10/3/07 Felt great! 2 units of blood, potassium and magnesium – awake all day. Good visit with Hannah and Jabrila.

10/4/07 Felt great. Walked a lot, developed rash on my neck – doctor prescribed cream. LP today at 3pm, laid around-no headache!

10/5/07 Changed central line removed and reinserted – otherwise feeling very good

10/6/07 Feeling good, lots of walking, numbers dropping – fatigue setting in, platelets twice, still feeling good.

And so began my next round of treatment. I had a rough start, but quickly got settled into the day-to-day experiences of chemo, blood transfusions and all that goes along with the continuing therapy for annihilating ALL. It always amazes me how resilient one's body can be. After receiving large doses of Chemotherapy, my body tended to react with extreme fatigue, headaches, and occasional nausea. The "anti-venom" for this was pain medication, blood and platelets, anti-

Detour

nausea drugs, drinking a lot of water, and walking. Yes walking. No matter how crappy I felt I was always encouraged to go at least one lap around the halls. This would usually turn into more as it did make me feel better. While lying in bed I had the opportunity to think about everything. This sometimes felt self-destructive as my imagination turned to the dark side. "What if this is the wrong treatment?" "What if this is all a big mistake and I don't even have leukemia?" As my thoughts would wander my trust would sometimes wane. Walking seemed to clear my thoughts and get me out of my own head. I often blamed my doubts on the drugs, because deep inside I didn't want to admit that I had such negative thoughts. But these thoughts did creep in and I kept them to myself.

My new room decoration helped. My nieces got together and made Prayer Flags for me. With David's help they sent out pieces of fabric, much like you would for a friendship quilt, and each person wrote a prayer or message on it. It was put together on a long ribbon and sent to me. I carried this to the hospital each time I went for treatment and hung it on the wall of my room. When I completed my treatment, I hung them in my yard, where it stayed for the next 4-1/2 years.

Detour

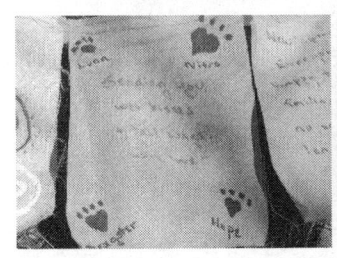

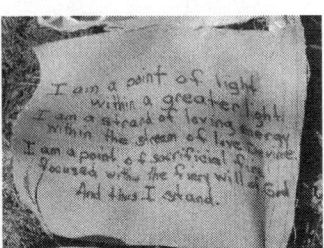

Written by my sister Jabrila, after a rather harsh lumbar puncture:

She looks so tiny, so small in the hospital bed. All curled up in a fetal position waiting, enduring, enduring pain, enduring the wait, a tear falls. I watch, holding her hand feeling useless. I want to take it all away from her, but it is not mine to take. This is her journey as much as I want to, it is hers. I can support her, love her, care for her but I don't get to rid her of cancer. I don't think she would even let me. Jane is so brave as I watch her being so still during an awful LP. I pray, I hold her in the light, I even

Detour

hold the doctor in the light. I was trying not to be angry that she was causing pain to my sis. So I held them in the light, both doing their jobs. She looked so tiny, so small, so brave being so strong. I am amazed day after day, LP after LP, bone marrow biopsy, central lines that have come into her life right now; and she endures.

I watch her become gentle, yet so strong; her spirit has grown. Her spirit comes out to embrace us all, to take care of us all, to teach us all to take the moment and live it.

Another LP, the last one was a "champagne tap" called that because it went so well; the last one! Reason to celebrate!

Jane, you are the reason to celebrate. Thank you for all you have gone through to live so I can get more time with you. Thank you for teaching me so much about the goodness in life, in Spirit, in love. Thank you for teaching me bravery.

10/10/2007

After a cool rainy night, it's a sunny day in SF. I'm starting to perk up a bit after days of weariness. My counts are very low (as they should be according to treatment) but I got platelets yesterday and that helped. 2 good things: I'm still in complete remission, meaning no blast cells, and this stay is shorter than I thought.

Detour

I should be home around the 18th for hopefully 10 days!!!! Jabrila went home and Kate is back. We spend our days walking around and watching movies. I'm getting to know a lot more patients this time and a chaplain started a Friday meditation session. I went once and it was very relaxing. So I'm here one more week and I need your help. I need new movie recommendations. I have a way to get movies, but am clueless as to some of the titles. Thanks.

David will be here Friday (yay) and Kate is leaving sometime this weekend. All is going pretty well, but I do miss my normal life. Hope you are all well and as always I appreciate all you do for me. On a sad note, my dear friend and neighbor of 25 years, Glenna, died this week. She was blessed to be surrounded by family when she passed. David and I will miss her, she was 85 years old. Blessing to you all. Love, Jane

Over the next few days I received GCSF which increases your blood cells and helps you recover from the low counts and had another lumbar puncture. As always we blessed each and every fluid that went into my body.

Bright yellow liquid, dripping slowly

Flowing effortlessly

Toxic doses they say, it looks so calm – so bright

Detour

I bless this as I've blessed the rest

It heals in its toxicity; again by taking away

Such violent final words to insure life

As I mentioned before, Nitro, my friend Beth's dog, became the blesser of all things that entered my veins. On one occasion we were watching movie on a big TV brought into my room when the nurse brought in the chemo. As she was hooking it up, my sister noticed that the TV screen was blocking Nitro's picture. She yelled," wait, wait!!" and took the picture off the wall so he could be "present" while the blessing happened.

I've dragged you through this without asking. Would you rather be at home, guarding the bookshelf?

During this visit, I met Chad, a 20 something guy who had recently been diagnosed with ALL. We became walking partners

78

and eventually friends. Leukemia once again caught me off guard as I realized how randomly it struck. The type of ALL we both had usually struck children, so as a 51 year old woman, this disease was a rarity, but a 20 year old healthy male? Was this something that had been brewing in his system since his recent childhood? So many unanswered questions. Chad and I reveled in the fact that we had the "good" type of leukemia. We were both told this. My guess is that it was one that had a definitive treatment; who knows. During one of his treatments he became quite ill. This was apparent in his disappearance. I walked by his room one day to find the door open. Chad explained that his kidneys started to shut down. He sounded really scared. He slowly ventured out in the hallway and told me he had just been talking to a friend about how wiped out he was. He told the guy, "I'm being lapped in the hallways by a forty something woman." That's the precise moment I fell in love with him, so to speak. There was something wonderful about getting a compliment like that from a young man. Going through treatment was making me feel old and slow. Forty-something felt pretty good!

Detour

My body recovered quite quickly and I was able to go home a bit earlier than expected, I felt quite good this time and hopeful that the following treatments would all end on a positive note.

10/22/07

Happy to be home

Hello everyone. It's Monday afternoon and I am happily writing from my kitchen! It's so good to be home. I didn't miss fall after all and am enjoying the cottonwoods and crisp air. I'm feeling good, still pretty weak, but I do what I can. (Maybe a bit more than I should!) I went to church yesterday and saw more people than I've seen in 2 months. It was a bit overwhelming, but very healing. Such a wonderful support. Today I'm just hanging out and relaxing a bit. I sneak out every couple of hours for fresh air and a horse fix. I will be home for about another week, but in November I'm home a lot more. I have to go back for two, 4-day treatments and that will end round 1, meaning I'm half way through!! End of November I begin the whole series again and will be complete in February!! It seems overwhelming sometimes, but then I take one day at a time, focusing on perfect healing and perfect health. I also think of all the support I receive,

Detour

not only from David and my family, but from all of you, and it truly does make the journey easier. So for now, Thank you all! It doesn't come close to my true sincere feeling, but it's a word of gratitude. I feel blessed by each and every one of you. Love, Jane

10/27/07

Hello everyone, It's another beautiful afternoon in Reno and I am getting ready for my walk. I have LOVED getting out and enjoying fresh air. I actually took a small hike yesterday at Thomas Creek with David and Nancy. It was so pretty and felt so normal. I did enjoy that. I've gone out to dinner 3 times this week and had lots of visitors and even had time to relax. Tomorrow (Sunday) I head back to SF for 4 days of treatment. I'll be back on Friday until the 11th, and then again be gone for 4 days. This time I am NOT taking my computer so I'll be out of touch until Friday. Hope you all have a wonderful week and that you enjoy the crisp days of fall. Have a fun Halloween too!!! As always, you are in my thoughts and prayers. Xoxo Jane

Detour

I went back to UCSF for the second-to-the-last treatment on Round 1 of the Linker Protocol. This was only a four-day stay and I shared a room. This is when I met DeEtta, who was just starting the same treatment for ALL. One of the nurses thought we would get along well, as DeEtta was recently diagnosed and I was 3 months into treatment. At first we didn't talk much, but once we started there was no stopping us. It felt good to share my experiences and talk about the fear and questions that came with a diagnosis of cancer, especially with someone who was going through it. I enjoyed "counseling" DeEtta, giving her a heads-up on her upcoming treatments and she seemed to respond positively. What I most liked about her was her optimism. Much like me, she chose to enter the experience knowing everything was going to be okay. She was quite religious and prayed daily with the hospital priest, as well as on her own. We roomed together for my 4-day stay.

The treatment was done intravenously with a less toxic drug called Methotrexate. I began with receiving a bunch of fluids and Bicarb to up my alkali level. The chemo was a continuous flow for 24 or 36 hours followed by a rescue drug which prevented kidney problems. One big difference was that my sister dropped me off in front of the hospital and I checked myself in. This was a huge step for me, and I felt very independent. I had a couple of visitors and read an entire book while there. It was kind of peaceful for awhile. The great thing about the 4 day visits was the chemo used did not make me neutropenic, meaning it didn't lower my blood counts. This meant much more freedom in eating and less worry about germs and infection.

My mom and brother came to visit and I will never forget how excited she was that she could finally hug me. "Baby, I've been waiting so long to do that," she said, smiling from ear to ear.

During this treatment, my hallway neighbor Dave was back too and I spent quite a bit of time with his wife, Lorraine. She walked the halls and often chatted with me. She offered to bring me a treat when she noticed I was without company and I happily accepted Snickers bars she bought for me. One evening she confided that her husband, Dave was not expected to live through the night. We cried together and she went back to be with him.

I spent the night thinking about death and how strange it was that, in the room right next to me, Dave was leaving this earth. I thought of the impact it would have on his family and was so deeply saddened. On one hand, he had been suffering so intensely that I imagined a sense of relief, but on the other hand, I questioned about starting life over without one's husband. I thought of David and my family and what my death would mean to them. I had obviously resolved to "fight for my life" or I wouldn't be going through this kind of treatment, but witnessing the impact it had on my new friend and her family strengthened my resolve to press on and champion my way through this ordeal. It wasn't just about me.

On my last night, which happened to be Halloween, I was lying in bed reading when the whole room started to roll. It was such a strange sensation and at first I thought "this medication is really making me feel strange." Within a second or two I realized it was an earthquake. Wow, I'm in San Francisco experiencing an earthquake! The floor seemed to roll and sway as I lay there wondering if I should get out of bed or do something. But what? I thought about the evacuation process of an entire hospital and that truly overwhelmed me. It's amazing what can go through one's head in a matter of seconds. The earthquake didn't last long and then it was silent.

Detour

DeEtta was using the restroom at the time and when she came out I excitedly asked her if she felt the earthquake. Her response, "I thought that was you knocking at the door because you had to use the bathroom." I felt kind of bad that she would think I would be that rude, but overall we had a good laugh over it. I felt so hyped up afterwards I went walking the halls. Of course all those seasoned San Franciscans had little to no reaction. I found it exciting and a bit scary. Turned out to be a 5.6, which was one of the biggest ones I had ever felt.

10/28 – checked in IV of Bicarb to up alkali in PH

10/29 – Still acidic PH – 6:30 started Methotrexate drip

10/30 – Sleepy walked some – ultrasound of liver

10/31 – 6:30 am chemo ended – Lucovoran (rescue drug) for 20 minutes Feel good

Earthquake rocked the 11th floor!!

Detour

11/3/07

Subject: back again

Good morning everyone, I'm happily home again. We (David and I) enjoyed a beautiful drive on a beautiful 75 degree windless, cloudless day. David took bald pictures of me with SF in the background; something to look back on in my healthy, prosperous future. This last treatment was actually quite easy. I'm feeling a bit fatigued, but otherwise well. When I go back in a week it will be the same treatment, but I won't have to stay quite as long. Maybe only 3 days!! Then home 'til after Thanksgiving. The most exciting thing that happened was the 5.6 earthquake last Tuesday. What a roller! Something about being on the eleventh floor of a building makes the swaying and shaking pretty obvious. Some people in the hospital didn't feel it, but I was lying in bed at the time, so it was very noticeable. Another change for me was having a roommate. She was a very nice 70 year-old woman, recently diagnosed with ALL. We chatted a lot and I enjoyed her company.

I played "big girl" this time and walked in by myself and had no one stay with me. I love my family being there, but that independent feeling was good. Made me feel stronger and more normal.

Detour

Sadly this time I lost my first patient-friend. Actually his wife and I were friends, and due to complications Dave passed away yesterday morning. It's strange to be on the "other side" again where I can offer comfort and be the listener. As sad as it was, I felt more like myself than I have in months. It also served as a wake up call that some do not survive. I thought of his family and friends and realized the impact it had on them. He was finally out of pain, but his family was just beginning to experience theirs. I thought of my own family and what they were going through with my illness. So much uncertainty. As I've said before, what a journey.....

The concern for others in my life extended beyond my family and close friends and into my workplace. Prior to my diagnosis I worked at a Child Care Center as a Preschool Head Teacher/Coordinator. Together with my co-teacher Renee and assorted student teachers, we had upwards of about 45 kids. The day I left the preschool, I had no idea I would never return. I worried about the kids and their feeling that I abandoned them. Once things settled down and I knew I was going to be in treatment for a long time, I gave permission to the director to inform the families of my situation. They became a wonderful support to me also. Here is a letter and I

Detour

wrote to them during my treatment. (Butterflies are the preschoolers – Coyotes the Kindergarten class.)

11/7/2007- letter to butterflies and coyotes

Hi Butterflies and Coyotes,

I miss you all SO much and wish I could come and see you. I am still pretty sick and can't be around too many people at once. I thought you'd like to see how Teacher Jane looks as a baldy, so I am sending a picture. This was taken near San Francisco. I am on my way home from the hospital there, where I spend a lot of time.

Did you have a pumpkin patch? How was trick or treating on campus? I've been missing out on a lot of good stuff! I miss you all and would love some pictures and cards. I decorate my hospital room with them. They make me smile. Enjoy the picture. (It's ok to laugh, but I think I look kind of cool.) Take care and hug Sarah and Renee for me.

Tell your parents hello for me and that I miss them too!

  Love, Teacher Jane

PS: Thank you Alex Deadmond for the beautiful castle picture.

Thanks Tourston for the race car picture.

Thanks Lydia for sending me a card.

And yes, Jacob, you are still my friend.

Detour

11/10/07

Boy this week went fast! I'm heading to SF again tomorrow chauffeured by my brother-in-law, Wendell, who lovingly offered me a ride. My week at home has been quiet and restful. I saw a few friends and walked a lot. I made it 2 miles on Friday!

There's something to be said for these breaks. It really helps to rest and rejuvenate between treatments. This week should be a breeze! And the good news is I'll be back on Wed. or Thursday. I have a few new books to read and comfy clothes packed, so it should be a good week.

Detour

Each time I entered the hospital for the 4-day stays 2 things happened: my veins were hard to find, resulting in multiple pokes, and I had a pregnancy test. This always humored me as I was 51 years old, and I'd had a total hysterectomy many years ago. But still, it was insisted upon. A nurse named May, who thankfully was very good at finding my vein, used to tease me and we'd laugh about the pregnancy test. "If I ever grow another uterus May, we could become famous." To this day when I see her, she asks if I've grown a uterus.

Because I shared a room on these short stays, family or friends could not stay with me. My brother-in-law, Wendell hung out for quite a while though, and then asked if I wanted him to bring me dinner. Of course I answered yes, as anything is better than hospital food, so off he went in search of Chinese. Around 6:30 or so I began to wonder of he had gotten lost. He arrived around 8 with Chinese food in tow. He had been wandering around seeing the sights of the city. I asked him if he got lost and he confidently replied "No, I just didn't know where I was for a bit." I could relate to that. I'd spent the last 3 months not really knowing where I was, or where I was headed. I guess that's not the same as being lost.

11/19/2007

Subject: Gratitude

In the spirit of this holiday I would like to thank you, my friends and family, for your ongoing support. Every prayer, thought, deed, and card has had a positive impact on my healing. You warm my heart and fill me with smiles and laughter; and as you know, it's hard to feel down when you're smiling.

I am blessed with the faith of a healing Spirit, which so lovingly expresses itself as each one of you. I have hope that all faced with challenges will experience the kind of encouragement and inspiration I have received from you. And the strongest of these is Love. Thank you for loving me and know I accept this and return it ten-fold to you.

Happy Thanksgiving!

Love, Jane

Detour

11/27/2007 Subject: 28 days

Hello everyone,

I hope your Thanksgiving was great. We had such a good time. My entire family was together, a very rare occasion, and it was crazy good fun!! David was awesome in pulling it all together. Of course he had LOTS of great help from the family. Tomorrow I head back to SF for a 28 day treatment. My twin sister is driving me and staying for a week or so. Kate will come down shortly after that for a few days and David will visit on the weekends. I'm bringing a suitcase filled with books, videos, games, etc. to keep occupied. I should be home on Christmas Eve or possibly Christmas day. My computer will be with me this time so feel free to drop me a line when you get a chance. Forgive me if I don't respond right away, as this treatment round is rather harsh and some days are tough. Please know that I appreciate hearing from you though! I hope you all have a great time during this wonderful holiday season. Enjoy the lights and smells and of course each other. I'll be in touch in a few days.

Blessings to you all, Jane

Detour

Jabrila and I left the Sunday after Thanksgiving and headed for UCSF. I was supposed to check in the following day, so we headed to my sister Annie's house in Vacaville about 50 miles from San Francisco. This is when I began to understand the intricacies of getting a bed on 11 Long. It was never a done deal. Apparently my insurance company wasn't so sure I needed this second round of fun and frolic and had not approved my stay, so instead of going to 11 Long, Jabrila drove me through the Napa Valley wine country. It was quite beautiful, and even though I was stressed out about the insurance mishap, I enjoyed the day. We happened upon a place where we spent a lot of time camping as kids. It was a club my parents belonged to, but not a fancy place. It was more of a ranch with activities and primitive-type camp sites. It had changed hands and was now an equestrian center and more of an RV camping place. We drove in, despite the *Members Only* sign, and went to the office. Jabrila diplomatically pulled the cancer card, explaining to the woman in the office that we were on our way to UCSF and wanted to "re-live our youth" or some other maudlin statement, pointing to bald-headed me waiting in the car. She gave us free reign of the grounds for the next 45 minutes or so. We had a blast remembering all the fun we had camping, horseback riding, and creek walking with my mom. We both looked up at the hillside remembering how we went up too high and had to slide down on our bottoms; Mom included.

Afterwards, we ventured back to Annie's and headed out the next day, sure that the insurance fiasco had been settled. It had, but after we arrived in the city, we found out there were no beds available. There was a chance a bed would become available later in the evening and the scheduling nurse would let me know. Becoming anxious is how I manifested my stress. And I felt very anxious. This was becoming too much, and again, I worried that the treatment delay would alter my healing and cause the leukemia to return. Jabrila, sensing this, took me to the beach. We enjoyed a late lunch at the Beach Chalet overlooking the ocean. We enjoyed a glass of wine which was almost scandalous during treatment, but hey, what the heck. It was always so easy with Jabrila. She could read my thoughts and not overreact to them. We talked about how nice it was to drive through the wine country and laughed about adventures we had as kids at the "Ranch." I relaxed for the first time and truly enjoyed the experience of being with my sister and best friend. She had already proved to be my "perfect match" in case I needed a bone marrow transplant, but this time around it was not necessary. I did tease her though, saying she needed to take care of herself, as she was my spare parts kit. She preferred to think of herself as my wilderness survival kit.

As evening approached we decided to go to Union Square to see the Christmas lights. As we were driving there I got the call saying my room would not be available until the next morning. Again she sensed my impending anxiousness and told me to call her Goddaughter Tara, who lived down the peninsula, and ask if we could stay with her. I think she must have circled Union Square 5 times while I made phone calls and arrangements. "Well of course Jabrila can stay with us. You however, I'm not so sure," Tara joked.

I was glad to be treated "normally" and teased in this manner. Tara and her family were very welcoming as they would prove to be many more times.

The next day we headed to my available bed at 11 Long.

12/4/2007

Subject: snowflakes

Good morning.

It's now Tuesday and I am on treatment day 5. I had a bit of a delay getting in, but I now am residing on 11 Long in a private room. It's a raining day, but my room is brightened up with prayer flags, a beautiful lavender-toned altar, Christmas lights and red bell decorations, and white coffee filter snowflakes. When looking at the good things that come from questionable situations, I would have to say one of them for me has been quality time. I have spent more time getting to know others, at a deeper level than ever before. I don't necessarily mean spiritually or emotionally, although that has happened too, but even more meaningful to me that I have been given this chunk of time where I don't have a time limit. It's okay to hang out and talk for hours or just be with someone. My sisters and I spent hours yesterday cutting out snowflakes for decorations, visiting with nurses, and listening to music. It was very healing.

There was no discussion on where we had to be next or how long anything would take; we just enjoyed the day, moment by moment.

Detour

On the physical healing front, I am handling the treatments well and might even have a slightly shorter stay. When this journey began almost 4 months ago I experienced more "firsts" than I ever thought possible. I am now beginning to see "lasts." Yesterday I had the last dose of a certain chemotherapy that I will EVER have to take again. My chart is filled with the word "discontinued." It feels like I am on the home stretch.

I wish all of you well and hope you too can find, or make, some "time for snowflakes."

Blessings, Jane

12/17/2007

Good Morning all,

It's Monday and day 18 of my current treatment and it's going very well. I had a rough time of it for a few days last week but am recovering better than ever. The new rumor is I might even be out on Wednesday!

I had a nice visit with David this weekend, and my sister Annie and brother Tom too. I also met Trina, David's brother-in-law's niece. She is a wonderful person who lives in SF and has been a great help to us. Kate is on her way through the snowy mountains *and will stay probably 'til I go home! I hear I missed the first snow, but am told there will be more when I get home. A White Christmas???*

I'm finding it so interesting how quickly one can bond with another human being. Within a short period of time, under certain circumstances, one can share very personal and meaningful conversation. It happens here often and it is very healing. I've experienced it with nurses, who become like family, other patients, and family members of patients. I feel a sincere closeness, but it's only in the moment. It's not like we all exchange addresses and promise to write; it's different, hard to describe. What I do know is that each person touches my heart in a way that only they can at that moment. And what I hope is that I give back in a similar way.

Please know that you are in my thoughts and prayers often as I enjoy the bounties of the ones you send me. Love, Jane

It's so true how one can meet another person and share intimate details of what they are going through after only moments of conversation. We experienced this often, and not just with families of cancer patients. At the end of the 11 Long hallways is the Neuro ICU waiting room. We often saw families in there for days on end. We'd

Detour

smile. They'd smile back. There were doctors sharing information, lots of tears, some laughter, people of all ages and cultures eating a variety of foods.

One family in particular touched my sister and me. There was a large family whose aunt, mother, sister, wife - all the same person - was in the ICU and they were there supporting each other and waiting for news. They would watch us walk by and always smile. After a few times around one would come and talk to us. It was obvious I was going through treatment, with my bald head or a colorful scarf and dragging my BFF, sporting, just as fashionably, numerous bags of liquid solutions attached to a port in my neck. It started with "good job" or "looking good" each time I made my lap. Then more was added to the conversations as we discussed why each of us was there. We all had stories and shared them openly. We became particularly close with a sister of the ICU patient. I think she needed to talk with someone who wasn't part of the family. She also became my biggest fan, endlessly cheering me on and lifting my spirits. They were there for days. One day a doctor showed up and talked to all of them at once, in the waiting room. The emotions were very high and there was a lot of crying. I smiled at them and went back to my room.

Detour

Next time I walked around, they were all gone and didn't return.

Some of the encounters were brief and passing like this. Others were more reoccurring, especially when it came to other patients at 11 Long.

My hallway hero, Ron, was back and I stopped by his room to inquire when he was getting his transplant. He smiled gently and told me he wasn't as he did not reach remission. I said I was so sorry, not knowing what else to say and continued on, feeling his situation was dire. A few days later Craig, Ron's partner and my friend, came to my room to tell me that Ron was dying. He wanted to take him home, but Ron was too sick to transport. He was also receiving such good care in the hospital it made more sense to keep him there. I began to cry and Craig comforted me with a hug. I felt so bad and sad and guilty that Craig was comforting me instead of the other way around. Craig understood and realized that as a patient, it was very daunting for me to hear this news. I couldn't imagine what he was going through. The two had shared a lifetime of love and partnership, and Craig was witnessing the love of his life disappear. I was truly heartbroken for him. We talked for a short while and he left me to my own thoughts while he carried his out the door.

The night before Ron died, Craig asked me if I wanted to say good bye. This was very new to me, as I really didn't know them other than our times at the hospital together and hadn't ever said goodbye to someone I knew was dying. So we walked into Room 1163 where Ron was sleeping. The nurse asked me to put on a mask and gloves, and Craig told Ron I was there. Ron looked up at me and said "Hi Jane" and drifted back into his slumber. I held his hand for a few minutes and said a blessing in my head. I thanked Craig and went back to my room. The next morning the solarium room was packed with people, bringing food, supporting each other, crying and hugging, sometimes laughing. I knew they were Ron's friends and family. Later in the day, Craig found me in the hall to tell me Ron had passed during the night. Kate was with me and we all wept and hugged. After Ron's death, Craig came back to 11 Long on several occasions to visit me. To this day we are still in touch.

Detour

Craig and me

12/20/2007

Subject: Home for the holidays

Hello and Happy Solstice! Just letting you know I made it home on Wednesday and am happily recuperating. Thanks for all the good wishes. I wish you all the best as the light grows brighter and the days grow longer. Love, Jane

Ps I'll be home until the 27th!

And I returned on the 27th, spending New Year's Eve on 11 Long. Two things I remember about that night: One, that Dr. Patrick said he'd drink a tequila toast for me at midnight (which I found out later he actually did – what a great guy), and two, my sisters came to eat Chinese food and watch the movie *Hairspray*. We asked the nurses to recommend a Chinese restaurant and all seemed to agree on the same one, which wasn't far. Kate went and got us the best Chinese food we'd ever eaten, and we watched the movie together. It was fun to relax and enjoy good food and each other's company. We celebrated New York New Year at 9 pm with silly hats. We toasted with ginger ale and Annie went back to Vacaville. Kate stayed the night and I don't think we made it to San Francisco New Year's.

To prove that I had too much time to think, I calculated the 100th day I had spent in the hospital since I first came to UCSF. I realized this number was strange, as time had become immeasurable.

Regardless of time, all was going as planned for round 2. I spent most of the week nauseous and tired, slept a lot, ate a little, and on day 8, I started to feel human again. I walked laps, read a bit, watched TV, and slept. A big storm hit and the rain was unbelievable.

On the 9th day the power went out and we were on backup power. Shortly after that my sister Jabrila and her husband, Wali, came and offered much entertainment through conversation and playing cribbage. At one point Wali looked at me and said "this is fun." I thought, well I'm so glad to offer you this opportunity. Proof that as humans we don't take time to just hang out. I felt pretty good

Detour

through this treatment. My counts dropped fast, so I got pooped out quickly, but otherwise felt good. I had a couple of minor setbacks, but nothing to "write home about," as they say.

I finally got a room with a view. Until now I looked onto a hillside of eucalyptus trees, which was very calming and peaceful. During this stay my room was on the other side of 11 Long, looking out over Golden Gate Park, the GG bridge, the north bay, and as far east as the Transamerica Pyramid. I could see both the San Francisco bay and the Pacific Ocean, when it wasn't raining, and the waves crashing on the shoreline 5 miles away. I was always surprised at how much time I spent just staring out the window. My room was pretty big and bright. And the prayer flags hung on the wall. I read them daily, with gratitude. Kate told me the Tibetan tradition is to hang them outside so the prayers can go with the winds. I love that. When I got home I planned to hang them in my yard. I told my niece, Noora, this and that my concern was they would get all weathered and ratty looking. She reminded me that by the time that happens, my treatments will be done and all this would be behind me. Profound reminder. (Thanks Nor.)

Detour

Chad was there during this visit and again we walked and talked, comparing notes and getting to know each other. We both had a profound fondness for the nurses and felt so comforted in their care. At one point I decided I would like to write a book for people undergoing lengthy hospital stays. It was to include how to alter your t-shirts to make picc lines more accessible. That way we could wear real clothes. The trick to wearing this was that you had to pull the T-shirt up over your legs, like a skirt. It was well worth it, not to have to wear a hospital gown. I even made a shirt for Chad so he could model how it looked.

Chad modeling the accessible T-Shirt

Near the end of this treatment I once again received GCSF to increase my blood cells. I was warned that it might cause bone pain, but had only experienced this mildly. Late one night my back began to ache and became so painful I couldn't lie down. The only position that was comfortable was standing, so I rested my arms on the sink counter and stood. The nurse came in and questioned what I was doing. I told her about the "bone pain" and she brought me some morphine.

I stood there awhile and when she returned to check on me, I was still there, telling her I felt stoned. She smiled and helped me back in bed. The pain was less, but still intense. The only comfortable position I could get into was lying on my back balancing on my forearms and heels, which in truth was not comfortable and I wasn't really on my back. The idea, in my mind, was to stay off my back while lying down. This was not very relaxing as one can imagine, so again when the nurse came in to check, she became concerned. She left and came back with a drug called dilaudid. This put me right out, but within an hour I was awake with pain again. The nurse then gave me more drugs and this time it knocked me out not only for the night, but well into the next day.

I have a vague memory of waking up and asking for a coke. I drank it and conked out again. My sister Kate showed up to supposedly take me home the next day. The day nurse stopped her before she came in the room and told her what was going on. She sneaked in the room to drop off her stuff and I woke up briefly, asking her to stay. I don't know why, as I was so out of it. I think I needed the comfort of her presence. Later that night I came back to life, feeling no pain, but groggy as hell. I slept through the night and both Kate and I were surprised when I was discharged the following morning.

Detour

The first of many important lessons I've learned:

~Take time for the little things and enjoy them. I don't think I will ever feel guilty about having a second cup of coffee while conversing with a friend. Whatever needs to be done will not go away, but the chance to spend quality time with someone special, may.

~When faced with challenges, it's not so much the circumstance as how you choose to deal with it. I would not have chosen leukemia or any disease for myself, but it showed up anyway. I consciously chose to make the experience as positive as I could and I have had some wonderful experiences.

~Humor does heal. Laughter is the best.

~Let others help. Being a giver is a wonderful thing, but it takes someone to receive. Being on the receiving end of so much love and support has strengthened my spirit and filled me with gratitude.

~Gratitude has become a spiritual practice for me. Everyday I find so many things to be grateful for. Even on the crappiest days imaginable, there is always something or someone to thank.

Detour

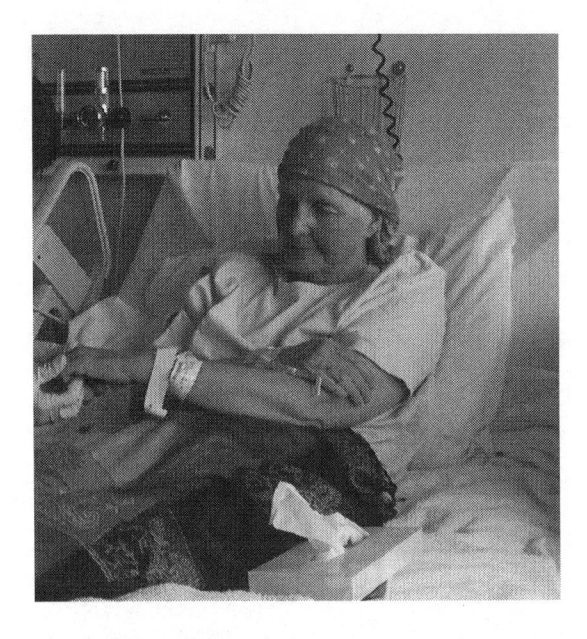

One of my last peripheral IV placements

I can see the light at the end of the tunnel. The better news is that I no longer think it might be an oncoming train!

As February slipped by and on into March, the 4-day treatments were going along well. I began to reach out to other patients more and get to know them on a deeper level. Sometimes when one meets a person there is an instant connection. Certain circumstances elicit this, such as sharing a hospital room or walking the halls of a hospital wing. I happily connected with two very different women during this visit, both sharing a similar situation and dealing with it in different ways. I met Doreen, an Asian woman, about my age who also had ALL. She was my roommate for 4 days and into non-traditional medicine. She had tried a variety of alternative treatments prior to this visit to UCSF including consulting a psychic, who advised her to seek a more traditional healing route. Doreen had a rather pessimistic view of her upcoming treatments and was quite scared. Because of my prior experience and belief in eastern medicine and holistic healing, I could relate to her uncertainties and our introductory conversation grew deep and meaningful at a quick pace. We discussed the pros and cons of western medicine and why each of us chose this route. Doreen appreciated my optimistic way and I respected her fear and doubts. Sharing my experiences so far with the treatments seemed to lessen Doreen's apprehension about her own upcoming journey. As her treatment was just beginning, mine was coming to an end. We bonded quickly and talked into the night.

During this same hospital stay I also befriended Billie who had just had her second transplant; this one being an embryonic transplant. In contrast to Doreen, she had an amazing outlook on life and a wonderful husband who was a constant support to her. We met

Detour

while walking the halls. Billie was quick to smile and share an upbeat conversation. She was a strength and inspiration to many patients and nurses. It was apparent, by the number of medicine bags she had attached to her IV pole and her slow awkward gait that she was going through major treatments yet she radiated good energy and wellbeing. Always a smile, always a kind word.

I soon learned that Billie also lived in Reno, and we vowed to stay in touch and connect when we returned to the real world. We longed for the day we could meet for lunch wearing street clothes and eat real food. And we did just that! The following summer we met for lunch and emailed back and forth. Doreen and Billie also became very good friends staying in touch through simultaneous visits to the clinic after their treatments were completed. After not hearing from Billie for a while, I called only to find out she became very ill and was sent back to 11 Long where she passed away. I was heartbroken when I called Doreen to tell her of Billie's passing. Doreen was too weak to make the trip to Reno for her service, but I attended with my sister.

I began to question why some people make it through treatment while others don't. At the funeral I was apprehensive about meeting Billie's family, yet I really wanted to pay my respects and tell them what an inspiration she was to me. I thought they would dislike me because I was still walking on this earth and Billie had moved on. Quite the opposite was true. They were very happy to meet someone who had survived cancer and was doing well. That gave me renewed purpose for taking care of myself and staying well. I did not hear from Doreen again after our conversation about Billie. The next time I called, her sister answered the phone and told me Doreen had passed peacefully in her sleep. Again with a broken heart, I called Billie's husband to let him know about Doreen. He said "I bet the two of them are having quite a laugh together up in heaven."

The quick, but frequent in and out of the 4-day treatments gave me time to wean myself from the long stays and the helpful nurses. Chad and his friend Donny were patients on the day I checked out. They had chairs set up in front of Donny's room and referred to it as the front porch. They'd play guitars, color in coloring books, and talk to the nurses. Talk about making the most of a bad situation. Saying goodbye to Chad and the nurses was bittersweet. I was emotional, excited, scared and relieved all at the same time. They had become like a second family to me. I felt so good about completing the Linker protocol, yet I was leaving my medical comfort zone to be

Detour

out on my own. I felt uncertain and independent; nervous and excited. I had such a mixture of emotions. "Don't come back! Except to visit," was a common response prior to leaving. So, on Saturday March 15th, 7 months to the day that I first entered the hospital at UCSF, I was discharged for the last time from 11 Long. I thanked the nurses, took pictures, walked away and burst into tears. I cried all the way down the elevator, hugging David, all the way to the car, and for a good portion of the day. It's the most I'd cried during this whole journey.

I celebrated the end of this intense treatment by walking across the Golden Gate Bridge. It was symbolic, very symbolic. The ability to walk away, leaving San Francisco "on foot", and having

Detour

David with me supporting me was an experience like no other. The actual walk was a bit difficult. The exhaust from the passing cars was very apparent, but the day was beautiful, a bit chilly but nice. Lots of sailboats and surfers crowded the water. I enjoyed watching it all.

The strange thing was that as I crossed I felt like everyone around me should be celebrating with me. It was such a BIG DEAL and I wanted to say "Hey World-I just finished cancer treatment! Celebrate with me!" But just as it was when I first got sick, I realized the world keeps going on, everyone busied up and living their lives, oblivious to my challenges and victories. As I walked, I wondered if anyone else was having a celebratory day or if they were trying to walk off some type of despair. Was it just another day in the life of...them? I looked forward to a day like that, a day when nothing about cancer or treatment or feeling good or bad is mentioned; a "normal" day of normal goodness filled with such normality that we subconsciously forget about such things and live just another day in "the life of Jane and David".

Detour

David and me on the Golden Gate Bridge

For my sisters, who could not be there with me to celebrate

Detour

I think it had not yet completely dawned on me how big this was, but I knew that I was living in constant gratitude for all of those who helped me through this time. I am still amazed and awe-struck by the amount of love, prayer, thoughtfulness and care I received during that 7 months. Thank you seemed the "tip of the iceberg" as a way to show my heartfelt gratitude, but at the time it was all I could think to say.

August 13, 2008

Hello Friends,

One year ago today I was diagnosed with A.L.L. and I can't help but think about all that has happened in that time. There have been a lot of lessons learned, by us all, prayers answered, faith renewed, unanswered questions; the list is really endless. But through it all I was and am still joyous to have had the support of all of you. It takes a village – oh yeah that's child raising – but still, you get the point.

In one year I learned that there are no guarantees

Life throws curves; how you handle them is what matters

Life is fragile – be gentle with it, be kind, live each moment – endure, embrace

Even the challenging moments cease and the great ones never last long enough

Detour

Love them all

Learn from them

Share them

Embrace them

Keep some for yourself

Rest – it's how we recharge

Give of yourself

Allow yourself to receive - its God's way of letting us know we're not alone

Laugh – especially at yourself

Cry

But most importantly Love.

Thank you for being in my life.

Blessings, Jane

Throughout this entire experience, I couldn't help but wonder how others coped with my situation. They, for the most part, put on happy faces and went along for the ride, but I know deep inside the trauma and scariness of this must at times feel unbearable. I started thinking of them as the true survivors. And, carrying on tradition, I found myself writing about my gratitude.

Detour

The True Survivors

The true survivors never had an IV stuck in their arm or a central line in their neck

Yet they felt every drop of fluid that entered each port.

They never had a Lumbar Puncture or a Bone Marrow Biopsy, yet they calmed the ones who did without flinching – smiling passively through each poke, scrape, and pain

They did not spend days on end in a hospital bed drifting in and out of sickness, discomfort and sleep

They stood guard, protecting, encircling

Hopeless to feel what they wanted to; what the other person was going through

They would take it away if they could, even take it on themselves

And for this unconditional bravery they are thanked, but not honored as the other kind of survivor.

You have survived the world of unknowns; yet you embraced it, gave up your time, your work, your family to stand guard and listen to things patients can't understand and don't want to.

You kept yourselves together with fear that if you start falling apart the pieces may break irreparably.

Detour

You are the honored ones; the ones who feel no need for honor; for your part in this is painful, and you maintain strength.

What you go through is nothing compared to the one who is sick

Untrue; it is everything.

Being on the outside looking in is difficult. You dealt with facts, but couldn't know the emotions, as they are hidden from you making it even more difficult.

I hold you in my heart – in my highest esteem because you are the true survivors.

Detour #3 – Transplanted-again and again and again…

On March 15, 2008, 7 months to the day that I was first admitted, I completed the Linker Protocol, in full remission and left UCSF. It was very emotional for me, like being kicked out of the nest, but better. After I got home I spent the next few days totally wiped out. I continued to gain strength over the summer, taking a couple of really fun trips, walking, resting, and enjoying life. In the fall I went back to school with the intention of finishing my degree.

I had a few minor setbacks, one being lung complications due to one of my maintenance drugs, causing me to have monthly chemo treatments in the local doctor's office. Prior to this, I was taking oral meds and had monthly check ups. The infusion center experience was new to me, as I'd had all chemo in the hospital. The treatment was a quick injection that took about 20 minutes total and other patients would comment –"out of here already?" or "wow I'm here all day." I'd just smile and wave, thinking, *if only you knew…*

In May of 2009 I graduated from the University of Nevada, Reno with a bachelor's degree in Human Development and Family

Studies. My whole family came, except Mom who was in a nursing home, and we had a big celebration. Over 70 people showed up throughout the day and it was wonderful. I spent the summer walking, learning to paddleboard, cutting firewood, being "normal." In October of that year I applied for a job that I thought was perfect for me. I was hired in November and, as it turned out, it was perfect. I worked in an office, but still in the early childhood field. I worked with fabulous people and learned so many new skills. I felt truly blessed by this job!

During this time I began to question my faith and reflect on my beliefs. I was raised in a "change your thinking, change your life" kind of atmosphere. When we were sick, we were probably thinking bad thoughts and if we changed them, our illness would go away. There wasn't a lot of explanation behind it all; it's just the way the universe worked. God created us as whole and perfect beings and it was up to us to keep it that way. My first round with leukemia, I kept a very positive attitude and didn't question why I developed this condition, only how to make it all better. Afterwards, when reality struck and I was thinking, "What was that about?" I began to question myself.

Detour

I spent months seeking others' advice and counsel, reading spiritual books, looking for answers. All I came up with was self-blame. What horrible things must I think about myself to develop this serious of a disease? Sometimes I would remember awful things I had done and feel really bad. How could I do this to myself? It was so much easier to look at it all in a physical realm.

I always thought of myself as a pretty kind person with a good spirit, so how did this happen? I was wracked with guilt and occasionally self-loathing. It was totally crazy, but I could get no solid answers.

So, I moved on and discovered it was a bunch of bull shit. We are all human – physical beings – living a spiritual existence. Some may argue against the existence of spirituality in everyone, but I believe its there and that some understand how to access it better than others. Some choose not to access it at all, but that's not where I'm heading. While the spiritual realm lies unharmed and perfect, our physical bodies have limits. We age, we break, we acquire disease, and without trying to sound trendy, it is how we handle these physical things that matter. What we do about aging reflects how we look and feel. How we handle the news of terminal illness, or even catching a cold, to some degree determines the outcome. My basic point here is I discovered it's always better to feel good about oneself. You have to live with yourself for this entire lifetime, so it's best to make it work. Do I get anxious and depressed? Oh yes, but I set time limits on my pity parties and try not to invite anyone else. I've had a lot of time for self reflection and realize that I am not a bad person and certainly unworthy of a disease yielded at me like a knife. So I moved on to figure out what does work, what I could do to make this experience better, what I could live with.

Many things challenged this, but I again rooted myself in positive energy. Even in the late winter of 2011 when my mom's health began to rapidly deteriorate. She went on hospice care in mid February and passed away on the 27th. Her passing was harder than I thought it would be and I started to feel physically spent. I went to the doctor and my white counts were pretty low. I tried not to panic, but I was a bit of a wreck. I had a sinus infection and was totally run down. I tried steroids and they helped a lot – so of course I'm thinking it must have been an inflammation.

In the summer when they dropped a bit more I wasn't all that concerned because I was feeling pretty darn good. I figured that the

Detour

bar was different, due to my past illness. I suspected something might be amiss, but went ahead as planned with my five-year remission celebration. I had a Thanksgiving celebration the night before Thanksgiving. I hosted my first ever Women's Circle and invited my closest women friends and relatives, the ones I thought would be into a circle such as this. Beth opened with an invocation, Jabrila called in the directions and together these wonderful women and I burned my prayer flags; offering them up to wind, to whomever else needed prayers, to the universe. It was a beautiful night and the ceremony was all I hoped it would be. The men joined us later as we feasted on all the good Thanksgiving foods that nourished our bodies and souls.

In late November I went for my five-year checkup; so excited to be sent off as "cured!" I was more than surprised when my doctor reported my white counts being even lower and that I was now neutropenic. What? There must be some mistake, I don't feel that sick. I think I heard that somewhere before.

So off I went back to UCSF for a bone marrow biopsy. Dr. Martin peeked in just afterwards and assured me my blood work was looking fine and he'd call me next week with good news. He and my local doc thought maybe I'd developed lupus or a form of arthritis.

Detour

"Yay, lupus!" what a strange and warped thought, but under the circumstances, it seemed okay. When I received a call from him two days later, I held my breath. I was at work, alone in my office. It was Friday November 30, 2012, around 11am. He said the results were not as good as expected and the leukemia had returned. He went on to talk percentages, numbers, even bone marrow transplant. I asked a couple of questions about treatment options in Reno and he said he'd talk to Dr. Conrath and call me tonight. I hung up the phone and broke down into sobs. My mind raced through all that Dr. Martin said. I kept hearing him say that the results were not as good as expected. I heard this over and over in my mind. I couldn't stop crying. How was I going to tell my family? How was I going to tell David?

I was so pissed that this was happening again. My life was settling down into a life I loved. I had a plan. David and I had a plan. I could feel it all slipping away. I was learning new things at work and finally felt like I had a career doing something I enjoyed, something fulfilling. I truly couldn't bear the thought of going through a lengthy treatment, upending my life and taking others down with me.

Linda, my office mate walked in and asked if I was ok. I told her no and explained what was going on. She kindly shut the door, letting me vent. She listened without crying, falling apart, or anything. She was just what I needed. I confessed to her that my biggest dread at that point was telling David. How would he react? How could he possibly go through this again when he barely made it through last time? She sat with me for a while and then I got up to wash my face and found I was shaking so bad I couldn't stand.

So, I went back to work.

I was finishing up some planning, entering information into a database, doing anything not to think about the conversation. Then I totally wimped out and called David on the phone. I just couldn't tell him face to face. He was devastated and kept saying "this is so fucked up." I had to agree. So after a while I gathered my stuff, asked Linda to talk to my boss, as she was on a call, and left. I was driving home thinking about everything and nothing. The radio played an Ed Sheeran song…"It's too cold outside for angels to fly." That's how it felt.

I went home and I will never forget the look of despair on David's face. It totally broke my heart. I spent the next five hours staring out the front window. I wasn't over-thinking or over-feeling, just staring. I don't remember thinking at all. Staring out the window became hypnotic and time just passed. Both doctors called later that night and both agreed that I should get to UCSF ASAP and begin induction chemo to get in remission and then have a bone marrow/stem cell transplant. I asked about the alternative, my prognosis if I choose to do nothing, which was something never mentioned the first time around. I would have about a one year survival rate.

It was Friday night, so I had all weekend to mull it over. I appreciated this time, as I didn't want to make a decision. A transplant seemed so radical to me, and I had yet to meet anyone who didn't have problems with theirs. Granted I knew only a handful of people, but their stories were not too cheery. This all seemed too much and I couldn't find a place where I could really wrap my brain around it, so having time was good. It also gave me time to talk to my family. I think they all suspected and feared that the leukemia had returned, as none seemed too terribly shocked. Our conversations were quick and informative.

During this weekend, I struggled to accept the return. Five years. Five years of life back to relatively normal. Five years of fresh air and health. Five years of being home. I dug through the past five years, emotionally and physically, rooting through records and desk drawers I had hoped to leave sealed. I found the unfinished manuscript of my journey, and reading it made the return of the disease even more palpable.

During my treatment five years ago I had a chromosome test to see if I needed a bone marrow transplant. While waiting for the results, two of my sisters were tested to see if they were a match. As it turned out, my twin sister was a perfect match, but at that time I did not need her stem cells. I could fight it as much as I wanted, but it didn't change the fact that I was sitting here five years into health, sick again.

I called my sister. I let her know I needed her spare parts, as we had jokingly called the donation in the past. I also had to ask her to cancel her trip to Patagonia that was planned for less than a month away. Other than talking with her I couldn't handle lengthy sympathies or solutions and I think my family knew that. They simply listened, told me they loved me, and asked to stay in the loop.

At the end of the weekend, I had decided to move forward, receive chemo and get a transplant. At this point I gave David an out. I knew this was going to be more intense than the first time, so I told

Detour

him if he didn't want to go through this again he could walk away, no questions asked. He gracefully declined, for which I am eternally grateful. So once again we found ourselves waiting for a room at 11 Long. We received a call Tuesday morning and left within the hour.

All those self doubts returned, and while still reeling and questioning my relapse, I went back to UCSF for 21 days to receive chemo. It was difficult to walk onto 11 Long again; so many familiar faces. The nurses greeted me with mixed emotions. We were happy to see each other, but not under the circumstances. Many were excited I'd been in remission for 5 years, saying that was a good thing. They greeted me with smiles and sadness, breaking the ice by giving me the "best" room. And it was – view of the city, the park, the bay and the church that lit up like Disneyland at night. It was also December, so colorful Christmas lights appeared at dusk, giving the city an even more festive look. It was all very familiar, too familiar. There were some changes of course, after 5 years, the good one being room service. I could eat what I wanted when I wanted and I could order a tray for a guest for a minimal charge. I could eat fruit and vegetables as they were prepared in the kitchen under neutropenic guidelines; meaning they were super clean. And so began my new adventure; one that lasted so much longer than I intended and one that would have me transplanted from San Francisco to Los Angeles and back to San Francisco.

The day after I arrived I had a port put into my chest for IV use, blood draws, and eventually the transplant. The insertion of this was much easier than the central line as I was pretty sedated and not uncomfortable. This particular port could stay in for a long period of time. When it was not "accessed," meaning no needles were inserted into the port, it was completely covered by my skin. This would make showering so much easier at home. I still had to have it wrapped at the hospital in order to take a shower, as I was never unhooked while in the hospital.

I then began the first of 8 chemo treatments over the next 4 days. After that I "hung out," recovering. I lost some of my hair, but not all. I had Gabby shave my head again, just like old times, so it was very short. The chemo came equipped with a lot of fluids, so I gained about 7 pounds in the couple of days. I was puffy, had a butch hairdo, and was still kind of pissed this was all happening again. Reminding myself, "its how you handle the situation," I decided to take a different angle this time. I was determined to treat it like a business trip, not get all hung up on the emotional part. Get in, get the job done, and get out. I even had my family and friends send business cards which I placed on the altar I set up for this round. I always had an altar in my hospital room during treatments. The pieces changed, but there were always a few meaningful treasures I could see and be with. It was comforting. A social worker told us about a website called Caring Bridge, which was a way to keep in touch with family and friends, much like the previous email list. David set up an account and again, I began to write.

December 15, 2012

In the past 10 days I have received 8 treatments of chemo therapy with the idea of getting back in remission as quickly as possible. After chemo the bone marrow stops creating new blood so my counts (white, red, platelets) begin to drop off. This gives the chemo a chance to clear the bone marrow and the blood supply of cancer cells. They will do a bone marrow biopsy in a few days to determine if I'm in remission. After that I get to go home for a week or so to rest. If all goes according to plan, I will be readmitted in January and given more chemo and maybe radiation to prepare for a stem cell transplant. This procedure is what used to be a bone marrow transplant, but they are now able to use donor stem cells instead of having to get bone marrow. The cells will be infused through my blood and start implanting into my bone marrow. It's rather like science fiction truly. It takes a few weeks for the new cells to grow and when they do I will have a new immune system and blood supply. This is a balancing act involving anti rejection meds etc, just like an organ transplant. It's pretty huge and quite honestly scary, but I am encouraged by the fact that I have a perfect match- my twin sister. Of course when I say perfect match I am referring to her stem cells. She and I are quite different in looks and lifestyles but right here, right now, I see her as perfect. An added bonus is that the staff here at UCSF is amazing. Recovery time is long and I'll have to stay near UCSF for a few months before turning my care back over to the local doctor in Reno.

Thank you all for showing care and concern. It means a lot to me. I'll keep this journal up as best I can...

Love, Jane

Detour

The days passed quickly with lots of hall walking, family visits, sleep, reading, crafty stuff; kind of a chemo vacation (hahaha).

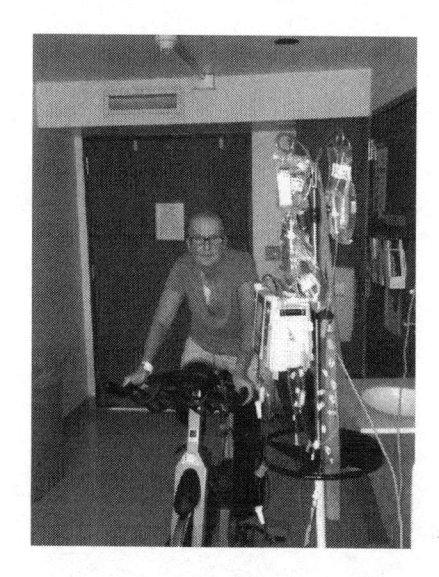

On Christmas Eve, Kate, Wendell, and David came and we dined in the solarium looking over the city, a five star view for a less than perfect holiday. But I was trying to keep it light, not attach too much to any of it except to get it over with. I went home just before New Year's to rest and prepare for the transplant. Part one, done; check. All was going according to my "business plan." First goal met; let's move on.

In the beginning of January, we went back to San Francisco for a series of consultation appointments. My biggest fear at this point was radiation: a complete unknown to me. The term Total Body

Irradiation was a bit more than overwhelming in my mind. It wasn't until my radiology oncology consult, shortly before my admit date, that I began to feel at ease. An intern discussed the treatment, assuring me that I wouldn't be "nuked" and that radiation was merely "high energy light." High energy light. That was a term I could live with. I have always felt a connection to light. The effects of lighting are very strong with me. I am deeply moved at certain times of the day or the seasons when the lighting is soft and warm. It's almost spiritual, so using the reference of high energy light somehow comforted me. When at my best, spiritually, I refer to the sensations as feeling the light from within.

I then met the radiology oncologist and she talked about side effects, explaining that most of her patients had relatively few. The hair loss is a given, diarrhea a probable, but nothing as scary and creepy as I was thinking. I think I tend to concentrate on the horror stories because that is what is sensationalized and that is what sticks with me. I felt comforted by both of these people. From there I went on to get measured and tattooed (little tiny marks where the machine would focus) and met the actual technicians who were going to irradiate me – oh wait, I mean cover me with high energy light. The machine was huge and I'd have to go in twice a day for 40 minutes, about 20 on each side, front and back, 9 times in 5 days. High energy light, high energy light; I made this my mantra...

Shortly after that appointment, I met with Dr. Martin, Lauran, the Blood and Marrow Transplant (BMT) coordinator, and a social worker for a consultation appointment that explained the preparation, procedure, and caregivers' responsibilities. David, my sister Jabrila, my brother Tom, and his fiancé, Robin were also there. There was a lot to cover. This was a bit hairy and scared the shit out of my toughguy brother. He and Robin sat there with the deer-in-the-headlights look. I had read the (BMT) binder, as had my sister, but my brother was taken a bit by surprise. The BMT binder was brought to me during the previous hospital stay. I was told to read it a little at a time. It was packed with anything and everything you ever wanted to know about a transplant, plus a plethora of information I would rather pass on knowing. I delved in slowly, trying not to freak out too much. Each day I'd read little more and when I felt brave, I'd ask the internist reality questions, such as "Do I really have to have radiation?" What are my chances if I stop right here and don't go any further. Can I live for a while with chemo every couple of months?"

Detour

The information overwhelmed me. I began to wonder if I should stop being so informed and just go in blindly and hope for the best.

At the end of the meeting it was realized that I hadn't had the much-needed bone marrow biopsy that determines my remission status. The meeting ended with a screaming headache and a desire to go back in time. My family was nervous and I couldn't blame them. We didn't talk much so everyone had a chance to process on his or her own time. I so wanted to get this show on the road and get on with my life. The following morning I had a bone marrow biopsy and then we went home for a couple of days.

And then we were back to SF for all the preliminary things one must do prior to a transplant. The first was a shot that was meant to thicken the mucus in my mouth which helps prevent mouth sores from the transplant and the after effects. I learned that graft versus host is a serious, yet treatable condition that is likely to occur as a result of the transplant. The new stem cells rejecting my body could be mild to very severe; everyone is different and it doesn't always happen. I wasn't worried about that, as I had a perfect match. I was to be admitted 4 days later to begin Total Body Irradiation (TBI) and I was feeling ready. Let's get going!

Detour

While waiting in the office, Dr. Martin came in which made me suspicious, as he doesn't typically give shots. I was sitting in a chair on the far wall. David was sitting next to an exam table, and Dr. Martin drew up a chair next to him. He had my chart in his lap and was looking at it. He looked up at us and once again stated, "The results of your bone marrow biopsy are not as good as I'd hoped they would be." It was then that he informed David and me that I was not in full remission. My bone marrow still had 50% blast cells and there had to be less than 10% to continue with the transplant, so it had to be postponed. I was stunned – no shocked. My brain set afire, and I couldn't think. I wanted to run out, give up, scream and cry, but I couldn't move. David looked like he was going to cry or maybe throw up. Doctor Martin then proceeded to tell us that I could go back into the hospital that day and begin more chemo.

"What are the chances it will get me in remission?"

"About 30%."

"What was it the last time?"

"About 50%."

Sometimes I'd rather not know these figures.

He then began telling us about a clinical trial in the Los Angeles area that was having great results without chemo; and it takes 10 weeks.

Jesus, I thought, 10 weeks in LA, away from home, postponing the transplant for 12 weeks. It was like Dr Martin was reading my mind.

"If you were my sister," he said, "I'd be driving you to LA right now."

So I boldly stated "Or I could do nothing."

Dr. Martin smiled, and without even looking up commented, "You're not there yet; besides I know where you live."

I love that man.

He left the room to call the doctor at City Of Hope. David and I just sat there not speaking; I don't think we could. When he came back in he declared, "Dr. Stein thinks you will be a perfect candidate for the trial. Give City of Hope a call and start setting it up. If you decide to take that route, you can be ready at a moment's notice."

All I could think was David's proverbial "this is so fucked up." I felt not just the rug was pulled out from under me, but that the whole world was spinning away and leaving me there hanging.

Detour

We left the office and went to the parking garage where we sat in the car and cried.

January 15, 2013

We are currently in a holding pattern with my treatment. I was due to begin the transplant process this week but unfortunately I am not yet in remission. There are a couple of options, one of which is a clinical trial in southern CA at City of Hope. I will know more by next week at this time. In the meantime, I'm enjoying being at home even with these crazy freezing temperatures. I'm grateful to all who are holding me in their thoughts and prayers and to our wonderful neighbors Deb and Mike for taking care of the animals, plants, and house each time we have to leave. And to Beth for filling in for them, bringing me food and making me laugh. I am blessed with a very giving and supportive family for whom I am grateful. This would all be a lot harder without their support. For now there is really nothing for anyone to do, but in the future David and I will call on you as needed. So be careful with your offers! Ha-ha. We will keep this website updated as much as possible via David and Kate.

Detour

My life seems to have a series of doors that open and close; paths that wander in different directions without obvious rhyme or reason. Some lead to road blocks and when they do, new pathways open and I tend to be guided down the right ones, in spite of myself. On the way home the next day, I received a call from the doctor in charge of the clinical trail at City of Hope. He asked if I had any questions and gave me his cell phone number so I could call back when I got home. I was pretty impressed that a doctor would not only call me personally, but leave me his cell number. I started to consider this crazy option.

After my initial refusal to go to LA for 10 weeks, (never say never), I went to LA for a consult. My insurance company okayed the consultation, so we figured it was best to check it out and hope they'd approve the clinical trial, if it came to that. Something about being involved in a clinical trial intrigued me. It seemed a win/win situation – a better chance of remission and hope for future cancer treatments without using chemotherapy. I do admit though, I was very unhappy at the beginning. Between the stress of dealing with medical insurance, the postponement of the transplant, and the thought of being away from home for so long, my anxiety level skyrocketed. All

Detour

the while I kept telling myself to be grateful for this opportunity, this was yet another detour that sent me down this new path. It was all pretty hard to understand.

From the moment we arrived at City of Hope, David, Jabrila, and I felt – without meaning to sound corny – hope. The grounds were beautiful, even in January, and the employees treated us like we were in a five star hotel. A true understanding of what patients are going through exists there and it showed in the peaceful atmosphere and the kind and caring service.

Jabrila and me upon or arrival at City of Hope

Quick note from Kate: Jane, David & Jabrila arrived at City of Hope this morning for consult. David sent this lovely photo of the twins. This journey

Detour

has taken them from the sub zero temps in Reno to a 68° day in LA! More updates to come. Kate in Alpine Meadows (current temp 7°)

After a lengthy consultation followed by yet another bone marrow biopsy, multiple tests and a lumbar puncture, we went away feeling pretty assured that I would be accepted into the trial. We left with the hope that I would be admitted the following week and begin treatment. It all depended on insurance coverage.

I began to realize that this part of the journey was going to be different. I was so trying to remain positive, but inside I was still pissed. I really did not want to do this. I was overwhelmed, apprehensive, not to mention anxious. I arrived on a Thursday with Jabrila and David, still not knowing if I had insurance coverage. Dr. Stein admitted me that day because I was experiencing fatigue, and the blast cells in my marrow had increased from 50% to 85%. This was unsettling to say the least. So off we trotted to admissions, then to the 5th floor of the Helford Hospital. My new home for the next 17 days was big and roomy, but I was not impressed. My feelings of not wanting to be here soon erased the hopeful feeling I had upon first entering. I saw the view and thought back to 11 Long, a view of the city and Golden Gate Park, eucalyptus trees, as I headed toward the tall window in the corner of the room. I looked out my new window and saw parking lots and rooftops, the 605 freeway, and a cement factory. I really did not want to be there. On the bright side, it did offer lots of natural light and I could see a lot of sky. Always lookin' for the bright side…

The nurse assigned to me was a character and all three of us really appreciated his sense of humor. Maybe it wouldn't be so bad. David got a hotel room and Jabrila spent the night; she actually stayed for another week and I was so thankful for that. The next day David had to leave and we still didn't have the insurance approval for the clinical trial. I was so anxious and out of sorts, I could feel myself falling apart. David left quickly and my insecurities began to set in. Maybe he was reconsidering his "out" option. Maybe this was too much to handle. Nothing seemed to be going right, and I wasn't sure how much more I could take. Dr. Stein himself called the insurance company and really advocated for my case. On Friday afternoon he informed me that we were a "go". Treatment would start on Monday, as there were preliminary things to do, (picc line insertion, IV fluids, pre meds, etc).

So I chilled.

Jabrila and I spent the weekend doing crafts and watching movies. She left for a few hours each day to get outside and walk around the city of Duarte, where the City of Hope was located. I lived vicariously through her Duarte adventures.

Clinical trial starts

January 23, 2013

Hi. Just a quick note to let you know I officially started treatment today. I have a new friend for the next 28 days in the form of a pump in a pack. There's a picture of us that Kate added today to the Caring Bridge photos. The pump will run continuously administering a small dose of the antibody. It's so sci-fi. Thanks again for being a part of this with me. It makes for a gentler journey. Jane

Detour

As promised, treatment started Monday and that is when I met my new friend, the pump in a pack. It administered a drug called blinotumamab, which continuously flowed through a picc line in my arm. This was the antibody that would hopefully find those crazy leukemia cells and eliminate them, without the same miserable effects of chemo. The pack stayed with me 24/7 for the next 28 days. The first dose was relatively small. While sitting by the window in our newly designated craft area, I began to feel chilled. I pulled a shawl around me but couldn't get warm so a nurse brought in a heated blanket.

Detour

I'm pausing here to say one of the greatest comforts – no, luxuries – in a hospital is a heated blanket. I vowed to put blankets in the dryer before using them at home because the sensation of warmth and coziness was unmatched. However, on this occasion, I could not get warm and started to shiver. I figured I was getting a fever and indeed I did. This was to be expected, but the amount of attention brought on by this fever was not expected. Dr. Stein came in and ordered pain meds for the headache that accompanied the fever and started me on steroids, Right away! The nurses and especially the nurse assistants were so kind and caring. They checked on me continuously and really tried to make me comfortable. The effects of the drug were short-lived and by Friday I felt fine.

February 3, 2013

Hello and happy Sunday. So far the treatment is going as planned. I had fever, chills, flu like symptoms-all to be expected. I contracted a bacterial infection, too, but being in the hospital I'm well taken care of. The doctors tell me it all means the drug is doing its job. The people here at City of Hope are very helpful and friendly. If only I could coerce one of them to take me outside to enjoy this beautiful weather... Tomorrow the dose of Blinotumamab (the antibody drug) will be tripled. It will stay there for the rest of the treatment, running continuously. My sister Kate will be here Tuesday. She will stay here at the hospital until I'm discharged the following week. They have an outpatient village where we will stay after discharge. I'll go to the clinic every other day, but will be allowed to get out and about. I'm really looking forward to that. Thanks again for writing in the guest book. I really look forward to reading it. Blessings to you all. I'm grateful for each of you in my life and for sending thoughts and prayers my way. Happy Trails, Jane

The next week they tripled the dose, which was the standard protocol for this immunotherapy treatment. At some point here, Jabrila left and Kate arrived. After a couple of days on the higher dose, I spiked a fever again, this time accompanied by a worse headache. I was given more steroids, which made me feel better, but had to spend yet another weekend in the hospital. This marked another great disappointment. I was SO ready to get out of that room and breathe some fresh air. I felt grouchy and anxious. Kate and I passed the time playing scrabble and other word games and watching movies.

Detour

Here with my Sis

February 8, 2013

Sitting here at City of Hope with Jane watching the clouds, playing Scrabble, reading, catnapping. We were hoping to be at the Village but a bout of fever & headache prevented our move. Jane is feeling better & on steroids which seem to help her, & now I can't keep up! These are all expected side effects (except for me not keeping up) and mean the antibodies are doing their job, Yay! Wandering the grounds here you find unexpected hidden benches & small gardens everywhere. Can't wait to walk around outdoors with Jane. Maybe Monday...Kate

Each day a nurse would come in and have me write *sweet as apple pie* on a piece of paper. This was a check to make sure I wasn't having any neurological complications. Not sure where they came up with that, but I found it humorous.

Detour

On Monday I was good-to-go and released as an out-patient to The Village. The Village is on-campus housing for patients like me, who live too far away to come in to the clinic often, in my case every other day, to have the pump changed and necessary blood work completed.

I felt very good upon leaving the hospital, so different from my previous chemo experience, but the change of environment was startling to me. In my excitement to leave I thought for certain that I'd just walk right over to The Village, no problem. After being wheeled out, I stood up and breathed that wonderful fresh air I had missed. Even in east LA it was great. What I didn't realize was how weak I had become. I walked everyday, usually twice a day, in the hospital halls, but maneuvering steps and carrying bags? Wow, what a wake up call. It's amazing how you can feel so great in one environment and then go to another, with say, steps and a suitcase, and it changes everything.

Needless to say we took the shuttle to The Village. The room was a small studio apartment with 2 beds, 2 chairs, a small kitchenette with a table, and a bathroom. The dressers were knotty pine as were the floors to give it a homey feel. After 17 days in the hospital, it felt very homey. Again, I was so surprised at how weak I'd become. Thank goodness I had Kate there to help me unpack and go shopping. The greatest thing about this particular unit was it had lots of sun. I had become addicted to sitting in the warmth of the sun and found it very healing. Not to mention that it was February and southern California was having terrific weather. In the late afternoon it came through the windows and even that was a treat. The tricky part of staying at The Village was that I had to have a caregiver stay with me all the time. In Los Angeles. I'm so blessed by an adventurous and giving family. My sisters and David took turns and covered both hospital stays without me being involved in the details. Bless them.

Detour

February 11, 2013

In our bungalow at Hope Village! I'm drinking wine & Jane's making me dinner, dog show on TV...Life is good. Jane is officially happy! Day off tomorrow. No nurses at 430am, no blood work, no appointments...
Kate

Kate took me on short walks around the campus daily. The grounds were amazing, filled with gardens, sculptures, trees and flowers; truly a well thought out facility. Everywhere presented itself as a place of beauty, peacefulness and healing. A wonderful place for recovery. There's something to be said for whole body healing. The doctors can do what they specialize in and make your body better, but your mind and spirit are so much more of the equation. How you deal with what you're dealt, and how your attitude expresses those feelings, can make a huge difference.

City of Hope really promotes the healing of the mind, soul, and body simultaneously, and it shows in the beauty of the surroundings. There is a large gate on the grounds with the following inscription:

Detour

There is no profit in curing the body if in the process we destroy the soul.

I felt very fortunate to be brought to this wonderful place where the attitudes of healing matched my beliefs. Another bonus was the discovery of the local Mexican market and bakery. It was within walking distance and we quickly became addicted to pan dulce - yummy bakery treats.

Once David arrived I could go places. Neither Jabrila nor Kate had a car, so with my doctor giving me sightseeing advice and permission to do so, David and I ventured out. We went to museums and gardens and even to a fun restaurant. I was feeling better each day, so a couple times a week we'd head out for an adventure.

Detour

True Confessions

February 20, 2013

Ok. Just in case anyone out there is feeling at all sorry for me, it's time to get over that. David and I have discovered LA sightseeing on my non-clinic days and I have to admit we are having a blast! We spent Saturday touring the Huntington Library and the LA County Arboretum. There is a photo from the Arboretum that I posted over the weekend. Both were beautiful and the weather was amazing. Today, a cool 60 degrees, we went to The Norton Simon Museum in Pasadena. It was fabuloso!! We saw paintings and sculptures by very famous artists (we knew they were famous because even we recognized the names) and an Asian exhibit with pieces from the year 150. The featured artist was Van Gogh, but there were also a lot by Picasso and Degas, who is my new favorite artist. The ballerina pictured is one of his works. Her skirt and hair ribbon are fabric and I thinks she's beautiful. After the museum we went to a way-yummy

Detour

restaurant, yes a brew pub of course, and ate delicious food while looking out over Colorado Blvd. Pretty fun and definitely a culinary delight. So that's what I'm really up to in Southern California. Tomorrow and Saturday are clinic days so who knows what Friday and Sunday will bring. Monday is my last day of treatment for part one! I will be disconnected from my pump in a pack, have a bone marrow biopsy and some other stuff, then head home Tuesday for 10 days. The results of the biopsy will indicate if I am in remission; keep your fingers crossed... After the 10 days I'm back here to repeat the treatment, which is the protocol for this clinical trial. So there you have it, full disclosure. As always, thanks for your guest book entries. It's so fun to read them. And I appreciate your good thoughts and prayers. Best wishes to you all. Love, Jane

Detour

On my last day at City of Hope I had a bone marrow biopsy, a lumbar puncture, various blood tests, and best of all the picc line removed and the pump in a pack disconnected. I felt like crap, but in the back of my head I felt a sense of freedom. We left the next day, homeward bound for 2 weeks. While at home we received the news that the drug had indeed done its job and I was in remission. All was looking very good. I was so jazzed about the clinical trial and the positive effects it was having on me. I was feeling hopeful, not only for myself but for others. The altruism in me was genuinely elated. And if this wasn't enough, I would go into the transplant feeling strong.

On March 8th, my friend Beth drove me back to City of Hope. I was admitted the 9th and started treatment on the 10th. This time there was no reaction, so I was able to leave the hospital in 4 days. Beth left and Jabrila showed up the day before my discharge to The Village.

Remission feels good

March 12, 2013

Hello, I am back at City of Hope and started my treatment this afternoon. I am currently here by myself, which is fine except for the high dose steroids and no one to talk to. I'm feeling very good today. I was reflecting back to the last time I went into remission. It was shortly after being diagnosed so I was just beginning the crazy amounts of chemo and procedures and never got to appreciate how good it feels. I am appreciating that now. If all goes well as anticipated, I will be in the hospital for only 3 days, then off to The Village again. I am here for about a month and then home for less than a week, as my transplant is scheduled for the end of April. No rest for the wicked...

As for now, I am walking daily and resting up so I can go into the next phase as healthy as possible. Not wanting to sound preachy, but ... it really does pay to be healthy when you get sick. I really believe that healthy habits (good foods, exercise, and positive attitude) have contributed to the success of my treatments and the ability for my body to bounce back. Just a little food for thought. And for those of you thinking "don't overdo it" (you know who you are), I am not. I am resting, reading, playing computer word games, and being aware of my energy level to know when to stop or slow down. I am also participating in a 21 day meditation challenge online with Oprah Winfrey and Deepak Chopra. I call it chilling with Oprah and Chopra.

I wish you all well and thank you for caring so deeply about my health and wellbeing and the wellbeing of David and my family. Happy Trails, Love, Jane

My Village experience was a bit different this time. We had a lovely, secluded room, but this time I felt much better. I had been in remission for at least two weeks and I was getting stronger and wanting to do more. I also had 24 days ahead of me and that seemed like a long time. We again had nice weather and did a lot of walking and sitting in the sun. I took on the job of cooking, because my sisters came all that way to care for me, and I like to cook. I was truly beginning to feel normal. One day sitting with Jabrila, we were having a heart to heart. She was beading and we'd just eaten dinner. I began reflecting about how I thought cancer was harder on family members than on the person experiencing it, because there was always the uncertainty of not knowing what to do, or what to say. She listened and let me express my feelings about my appreciation and concern over what my family was going through. I was washing dishes and cleaning up, talking all the while. As I finished, she looked up totally relaxed in the moment of beading, dinner, pan dulce, CA sunshine, and said,"Yeah, can't you tell its killing me."

Detour

Breakfast

March 20, 2013

This morning I woke to the smell of coffee, bacon, and apple cinnamon bread. Yes, this is the usual morning routine. Then we meditate, do some stretching and exercise, shower and on to our morning walk. Clinic appointments, lunch, a little rest, then more walking. And we always end the day with an evening walk. And all the while the birds are singing and these amazing trees are blooming. I find it quite challenging being Jane's caregiver. I never get to things before her. Jane is doing really well; she is taking good care of herself and me. It is a very calm and beautiful environment here but for Jane there is no place like home... This is her journey and she will get home. In the meantime I will keep on walking with her, if I can keep up.

Happy trails to you, Jabrila

From Kate

March 29, 2013

I sit in the warm afternoon sun outside our bungalow with Jane on my last day of stay here at City of Hope. Reflecting on how lucky I am to be able to have shared this time together. It's not often we take the time to truly smell the roses and appreciate life's gifts. I am today. Lots of lessons, laughter, & shared moments. Jane is doing well - hard to be away from home for so many extended periods. My sis Annie & niece Hannah are on their way today. After chatting with others here I realize how great it is to have a big family who is willing & able to share the journey. Not everyone does... Keep those emails coming friends! Staying connected is good for the body & soul so say O & Cho. Weather is so perfect here, flowers amazing & being awoken to bird songs in the am pretty nice too! Not to mention the healthy meals cooked by Jane of course & pan dulce treats from down the street. As I head back to the still wintery weather in Alpine I'm wishing I could stay & Jane could go. For her there's no place like home.

The month went on with Jabrila leaving, Kate arriving, Kate leaving, and Annie and Hannah arriving…it was fun to spend a week with each of my sisters. I don't know if we'd ever do that on our own. Because I was feeling good and had clinic only every other day, we all felt like we were on vacation instead of going through cancer treatment and being a caregiver. On one such visit to the clinic, I was getting a blood draw, and discussing the clinical trial and my upcoming transplant with a nurse named Holly Bengston. I learned that Holly had a transplant 2 years earlier and was happy and healthy.

As the nurse shared her experiences, I was actually getting excited about my upcoming procedure. I had yet to meet a successful transplant recipient, and here in front of me was this amazing and inspirational woman telling me that everything would be great. This is the moment I actually believed it would be.

Me with Nurse Holly at City of Hope

Me with my sister Annie, niece Hannah, and my sister Kate

One week to go...
April 1, 2013
Good Morning,

It's a cloudy cool day today. And very quiet. My sister Annie is here now and busily working on her computer. I am between clinic appointments. My typical clinic day is getting blood work, waiting, seeing the doctor, waiting, and then getting the pump changed. All in all this takes about 3 1/2 hours. No big deal as I am right near everything. My doctor appointments are relatively quick as I am pretty low maintenance these days. My doctor saunters in with a melodic "Hello" and asks how I am feeling. We look at my blood work together and he says "Very Good" (in his Dutch accent) a few times and then we discuss sights to see in the area. He doesn't want me to get bored sitting around The Village... On Saturday, my sisters, niece, and I went to the Arboretum and enjoyed an outdoor day with trees, flowers, peacocks, etc. It's quite beautiful there. The Justins (David's family) will visit today and we're going to Pasadena to the museum. My sister hasn't been there and I think it's worth a second trip. My doc doesn't really have to worry about me getting *bored, or sitting around. And I am grateful I feel well enough to do these things!*

I'm continuing my daily meditations, walking, and learning to take deep breaths. My only discomfort is a really bad case of homesickness. So I hope you are all well and creating healthy habits of your own. I won't have time to see many of you on my next trip home as I'm off to UCSF pretty darn quick to get ready for and have my transplant. Thanks for being a part of this crazy journey. It takes a village...

Happy Trails, Jane

I was getting pretty homesick and was happy when David showed up to take me there. I ran into one of the hospital doctors in the hallway just before leaving and she commented on how great I looked. I told her my biggest discomfort was homesickness. She laughed and said,

"*That* should be our slogan." Again I had the same procedures on the last day – bone marrow biopsy, lumbar puncture – and felt pretty raw going home, but I was going home. No pump in a pack, no tethers, just me. And that was short lived. Less than a week later I went back to UCSF to start the preliminary treatments for the stem cell transplant.

Tour de California

April 16, 2013

I have had a wonderful 5 days home and enjoyed a celebration, a BBQ, walks, horses and time with friends. Mostly I loved being home; sleeping in my own bed, taking care of the critters, hanging out with David, etc. So now it's time to get down to business. I'm done at City of Hope and we leave tomorrow towards UCSF. It's our own little tour de California...It will all begin on Thursday with 5 (count em' 5) clinic appointments. Friday and Saturday I have one appointment each day. All preliminary things for the transplant. Things like shots to thicken my mouth mucus, inserting another port, blood work...I will be spending time with my brother this week, then some time in

Detour

Vacaville with Annie. Monday the 22nd is admit day and the first day of full body radiation or as I prefer "high energy light." It's all in the wording. I will receive 9 treatments in 5 days followed up with a high dose of chemo. The whole point is to annihilate any unseen disease along with my blood supply and immune system. That way the transplanted stem cells have a fresh start. Jabrila will be there too, obviously, as she is my donor, getting shots to boost her blood cells for collection. She will have her cells harvested (good word for a farmer) on the 29th and I will receive them the next day. Medical miracles, I'm telling you. Maybe more like science fiction. So after the transplant, which for me is likened to a blood transfusion, I stay in the hospital and recover. Within the next few weeks the new cells will begin doing their job. I will be in the hospital for 20 to 30 days, but then will stay in the area for multiple clinic visits over the next few weeks. The whole graft vs. host thing is new to me and I'll let you know how that goes as it happens. As for today, I'm packing, walking-probably in the snow- and reflecting on how lucky I really am. Doors have opened for me; friends and family showed up for me, I have a supportive husband and a friendly place to come home to. Leukemia is a set back; a bump in the road. Albeit a very large one! It doesn't define me or make me a victim, it is what it is. Time to move forward and then move on. Thanks for staying in touch, for thoughts and prayers, and for being there for me. It does not go unnoticed. Happy Trails.

Love, Jane

We arrived Wednesday night at my sister Annie's house in Vacaville, which would later become my home for 2 months. The next day we headed to UCSF for blood work, a Paliferman shot (to thicken the mucus in my mouth and prevent mouth sores) and a second consultation. Bridgett, a BMT coordinator, was kind and informative and really interested in the COH treatments. I was feeling less apprehensive in this consultation and ready to rock and roll. In truth, the sooner I got started, the sooner it would be over. She said the record for getting out of the hospital after transplant is 14 days. I was up for the challenge. Dr. Martin arrived and I asked him if I could hug him. I was SO thankful that he sent me to City of Hope for the clinical trial. He was really jazzed at my outcome so far and confident about the success of the upcoming transplant. I felt really positive going into the process; and I had a few days to process everything before my hospital admittance. After we were finished,

Detour

we cruised to Pacifica to see our home for the first month after the transplant. We then went to my brother's house where our camper was neatly tucked in his driveway. This was the beginning of "his turn" to be backup caregiver to David and overall watch dog. I think he liked that role, bless his over-protective heart.

100 days…

That's the number the doctors and nurses kept using when talking post transplant. After two more clinic visits and 2 more shots, I entered the hospital on Monday April 22nd. This was not day one, however; this was T minus 8. (Not sure what the "T" means…) As if the whole thing was not perplexing enough, they throw math in the mix. Transplant Day is Day Zero (not one) and Day one is the first day after the transplant. So, the 100 days begins on day one. Luckily for me it was the first of the month so counting from here on in was relatively easy.

On that Monday, David, Jabrila, Jabrila's husband Wali, and I all went to admitting and checked me in. Once again we took the elevator to 11 Long where I would get my treatment over the next month, give or take. The very first time I was admitted to 11 Long, a lovely nurse named Kari helped me settle in. I was a total wreck and she eased the process with kindness and caring. This time the same lovely nurse greeted me and treated me with the same kindness and caring. She also got me a room with an amazing view. We were all so happy with the view that it overshadowed all the things yet to come. That's one of the most important lesson I have learned: embrace the simple joys. If one moment is filled with any kind of joy, peace of mind or calmness, take a hold of it. It helps later when things aren't so bright and cheery.

I no more got settled in before I was whisked away to begin my first of 9 total body irradiation (TBI) treatments. I was taken by wheel chair to the basement and into a very large room with a very large machine filling half of it. I was welcomed by two technicians who helped me to lie down on a massage table set up on the floor. I brought a music CD which they put on as they prepared me. *Ain't Nothin' Like the Real Thing* played as they lined up a laser beam dot with the tattoo I received in January. A set of lung blocks were secured over my chest to block out some of the radiation to that area. The techs smiled as they left, closing the 8-inch thick solid door behind them. It was just me, the machine, and Gladys Knight singing with Vince Gill. The machine started at my feet and gradually made its way to the top of my head. It was kind of noisy, and as the week progressed I realized the rhythms of the beeps and could tell what would be next.

After 20 minutes or so, the techs came in and I flipped over onto my stomach, receiving the treatment again. At the end, they removed the lung block, helped me up and called for someone to wheel me back into my room.

I did this twice a day over the next four days, sometimes walking down to treatment, other times catching a ride. For the most part I felt pretty good the whole week. I soon learned the effects would come later. On the second day, my sister and her hubby escorted me down to see the machine. They looked a little shell shocked at the size of the machine and the room that held it. I think it surprised and frightened them a bit. For me, it was pretty much relaxing, listening to music and thinking of nothing as best I could. Basically, I meditated my way through radiation.

On my last day the transport guy was walking with me to the elevator, wheeling the wheelchair, just in case. We waited awhile for the elevator and a man appeared pushing a gurney with a medium sized blue bag on it. I inched towards it thinking to myself, there's a body in there. And it wasn't very big. I thought of the family of this person and the sadness. I started to enter the elevator with them, and the transport guy gently took my arm and led me to another elevator; much respect for the living and the dead at UCSF.

Moving on...

April 26, 2013

I can check total body irradiation off my list...yay!! And I'm feeling pretty good. Tomorrow is chemo as Jabrila continues getting shots to stimulate stem cell growth. Monday is her harvest day, Tuesday is transplant day. It's just like farming.

All this fun ended on Friday, and on Saturday morning a very cheery nurse named Byanca entered my room and announced that we were spending the day together. She had a "Mike Tyson" dose of chemo therapy for me that would take 4 hours to administer. She would be in every 15 minutes to check on me by taking vitals and making sure I was okay. I was forewarned about this particular dose and, again, tried not to think too much about it. I know there was antifreeze in the mix and that I had the potential of a horrific hangover when it was complete, but it was just one dose.

The nurse was available to me at all times, and my sister was hanging out, my brother too. So in it went. Lots of fluids too. And as promised, Byanca or one of her counterparts showed up every 15 minutes. There were lots of pre-meds to prevent nausea and allergic reactions and during the infusion I felt pretty good - at first. Towards the end I started feeling a bit flu like, so I took some more meds and slept. I don't remember exactly when the full effect hit me, but hit me it did. I felt like my veins were pumped full of lead, I'd been beaten up, slammed against a wall, and left on a cold cement floor. And this feeling lasted a very long time. I kept thinking, "I'm so glad I don't have to go anywhere or do anything."

The bathroom, which was a couple of feet from my bed, seemed like an eternal journey. The effects of being flattened by Mike Tyson were truly brutal, but did not last forever. By the next evening I was starting to perk up a bit and then came the diarrhea, a common side effect of TBI and one that was expected, but not very welcomed. As I confided that it was really not too bad, I'd hear "it gets worse before it gets better." Great.

Detour

For the two nights preceding my transplant, I lay awake thinking about how really huge this whole process is. My body was no longer able to produce its own blood and my immune system was deteriorating as I lay there. I kept thinking "there's no turning back; this is it. If I did nothing at this point my life would end."

But I knew it wasn't the end.

In fact cognitively I knew it was a new beginning, but still I sat with it. I felt the need to honor that which is rarely felt. I tried going deep in my soul and really feeling. But mostly I just sat with it.

No going back

April 29, 2013

It's Monday morning and I just walked my sister to hemo/dialysis, which is right around the corner on this floor. She's being prepped and readied to have her stem cell collection. It's really quite remarkable. I will be able to go in with her later on but because they give her a light sedative, she'll probably be sleeping. Words cannot express my appreciation of her and the ease of this process. She's so mellow and assuring about the whole thing even though I know how concerned she is. After the collection the cells will be counted and screened to see if they are viable (no doubt in my mind) and I will receive them tomorrow. It's such a big thing, yet the process seems so calm and lacks stress that it's hard to get a true grasp on the bigness of it all, for which I am grateful. Keeping it light is way good.

I am feeling pretty good today. TBI is wreaking small havoc on my digestive system, but it's manageable. This high dose chemo kicked my ass for about 10 hours. But by the wonders of modern medicine, I slept through quite a bit of it. The next day was better. So now my counts are coming down and my body is preparing for a whole new adventure. There is no turning back; it's all moving forward one step at a time. Tomorrow will become a second birthday of sorts. It's cool I still get to share it with my twin. As always, thank you for sending your kind words, thoughts, prayers. I absorb them daily and feel blessed by each of you.

Happy Trails! Jane

On Monday, two days after the chemo, Jabrila went early to the apheresis room to donate her stem cells. I walked the short distance down the hall with her. She had a hospital bed in the corner of a room that had a TV and a huge machine that would extract her blood, separate the platelets and stem cells, and return all other blood

Detour

products into her other arm. She was SO ready, it was inspiring. Jabrila had spent the last four days receiving neupogen shots to increase her blood cells. This caused a bit of bone pain, but Tylenol worked. I suppose I will never know how uncomfortable she really was, because she wouldn't say. That's how she is.

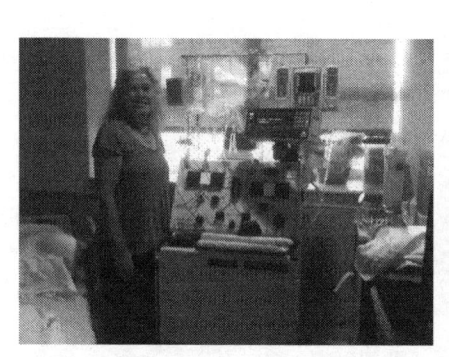

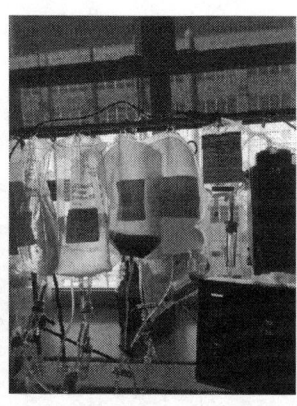

As I watched in fascination, the nurse explained what was going to happen - needles in both arms, slight sedations, etc - and then she kicked me out. I cried all the way back to my room, then blessed Jabrila, kissed the Buddha heart she had placed on my makeshift altar, and thanked the universe for her presence in my life. I stayed away for a couple of hours, then found out she was trying to stay awake to see me again, so I went back. My sister Kate and brother Tom showed up as well. Jabrila was watching the CARE channel and loving the photography. She lay in bed with her arm held stiffly open so the needle would not move. I looked at her and commented on how stoned she was. She said "No, no, I'm not. I'm just enjoying the pictures on the TV and feeling so relaxed." The nurse suggested a quick visit so she could rest, as that would make the procedure go more smoothly. We left the room, and Kate and I looked at each other and said simultaneously, "She's stoned."

By 2pm Jabrila had pumped out about 65 million stem cells. She was tired from the sedations and a bit out of it, but overall felt good. She and Kate headed out for a walk to the park and I hung out with my brother and rested. On the walk she received a call asking her to come into the clinic and get one more shot, as they needed her to donate more cells the next day. She'd already pumped out millions, but my doctor wanted to be sure there were more than enough and asked her if she could do a second day. Even though she was tired and sore, she was absolutely ready and willing to do whatever she needed to do.

When she arrived back to my room I offered her my bed so she could take a nap. She willingly accepted. A while later Doctor Martin showed up to check on me. I was sitting up in the chair and Jabrila was lying on my bed. He looked at Jabrila and then at me, smiling, pretending to be confused. It was pretty humorous and we had a good laugh. I loved how he praised her for her great job at pumping out those cells. He explained that that day's cells would go in the freezer and the next day would be added to the fresh ones. The transplant was on for Tuesday April 30th, 2013. It was really going to happen and April 30th would become my new birthday.

The day of the transplant Jabrila went to the apheresis room early again and I waited behind because I couldn't go too far from the bathroom. I checked in on her once to let her know why I wasn't there and she was fine with that. Her sedatives had kicked in and she was looking pretty relaxed. She had an awesome nurse and when I left they were talking about climbing mountains, my sister's favorite subject. I then knew she was in good hands. I hung out in my room, Kate came back, and then David showed up. We were all anxious but trying not to be. Jabrila finished around 2:00 again and went to get food with Kate. The waiting was a bit disconcerting, but mainly because so many people were involved. Yes I was getting the transplant, but my sister was such an integral part of it all, not to mention my husband, my other siblings, the doctor, nurses, etc.

Detour

Hurry up and wait; this had become a common practice. My stomach stuff abated for awhile and I was able to walk the halls. The nurses of 11 Long are so supportive and positive. Each one would either say, "Today's the day!" Or I would tell them "Its transplant day!" and they'd get teary eyed and cheer. The actual transplant was scheduled for around 4pm. At 3:30, my family sat around the room, David sleeping, Jabrila resting, Kate playing computer games and asking me questions. At 4:00, David startled out of a dead sleep. He looked at the time and said "Its 4 o'clock. Where is Jane's new life?"

As it turned out my new life was brought in about an hour later. It came in a little red cooler, just like you see in the movies. I couldn't believe it. Lauren, my transplant coordinator came in, as did a couple of nurses. Rei, who would be with me for the first part, explained the process, and the room began to fill up with family and staff. My family took pictures and sent blessings. It was all pretty amazing. This was real. The moment I'd been waiting 4 months for was here.

My new life, a new beginning, a cure; the little red cooler held so many possibilities for me.

Detour

When a child is born, my sister Jabrila makes a turtle that is beaded on one side and leather on the other. She fills them with herbs and often the umbilical cord of the child, should the parent choose to offer it. It's a Native tradition that Jabrila cherishes, as do the parents that receive this gift. Turtles are a connection to the earth. My nurse Rei was very excited about this because in her country, Japan, turtles mean long life. To symbolize my new life, Jabrila made a beaded turtle for me. It was stuffed with herbs and beaded in burgundy and green. The turtle's belly is sage green soft leather, like suede. As the first drops of cells entered the port and my body, Jabrila and I laid together on my hospital bed, turtle in hand. Lauren suggested that maybe we could put a drop of the cells on the belly of the turtle towards the end of the procedure. We all loved this idea. I felt so respected and supported by the nurses during this time. They honored my choices and never judged.

The nurses enjoyed that we made a celebration out of not only the turtle, but the whole amazing event, and did everything they could to support and assist in making it a positive experience. Doctor Martin walked in looking like he was ready to have a party. He was so happy and positive and literally lit up the room with his enthusiasm. He kept telling Jabrila what a great job she did and seemed genuinely elated over the whole event. Kate and David took a lot of pictures, and then Dr. Martin got to serious work for a few minutes after which he practically danced out of the room. It was so comforting to have that kind of energy from the person who was not only my primary physician, but who had been so deeply invested in my life.

My sister Kate told me that she walked out of the room just after him. Dr. Martin asked if she was a hugger and through tears she replied, 'Oh yes!" They hugged and he walked away doing fist pumps in the air. To celebrate my new life, Robin and her daughter brought me birthday treats and my family all sang Happy Birthday. Shortly after that, about shift change time, a group of nurses came in with a birthday cake and they sang me happy birthday. It was overwhelming, in a very cool way.

Things were quieting down when the second bag of stem cells began infusing, around 7:30pm. It was smaller, but I still couldn't wrap my brain around the significance of this little bag of cells. This process was SO huge on most levels, but occurred just like it happened every day. I thought about the science behind it, the many researchers who figured it out, the people who decided to be anonymous donors, my sister donating; it's all so amazing and generous.

David and I were hanging out alone in the room pretty much in silence. The silence was filled with peace, and hope, and to some degree fear. Near the end of the second bag the nurse asked if we wanted pure cells on the turtle, as she was about to dilute the cells with saline to get everything out of the bag. That was the goal, so very carefully using a lot of cleanliness precautions she disconnected the line and dropped a couple of drops of the stem cells onto the belly of the turtle. Because the belly of the turtle was made of suede, the cells beaded up on the top for a bit before absorbing into the leather. The stem cells looked like a dark amber bead as I held it, amazed at the power of that drop. I handed it to David's less shaky hands and together we watched as it slowly absorbed into the turtle belly, mixing with the herbs inside. The cells left a round stain in the middle of the belly and with it amazing experience that filled my heart with love, comfort, and hope.

Jabrila came in moments later, sorry she missed the event, but awed by our experience. Everything was okay with Jabrila. That's how she is. Missed something special, it's okay, glad someone else got to experience it. I am beyond grateful and past honored that her stem cells were my perfect match. Who wouldn't want that kind of goodness circulating and rebuilding one's body?

Update from Kate - a new birthday for Jane!

May 1, 2013

Amazing day yesterday on every level. Jabrila's harvest was plentiful 80+ million stem cells over the course of 2 days.

Jabrila, Dr. Martin and me

Truly the gift that keeps on giving... Jane received the cells in the late afternoon with blessings, laughter, great gratitude, love & birthday cakes! (One from family & one from all the nurses who came & sang Happy Birthday!) Lauren, her transplant coordinator, says "the cells will rush to the bone marrow like homing pigeons." There they will settle in over the next couple of weeks and begin to build a great new healthy system! Jane is sleepy today & experiencing the expected discomforts while her spirit & smile remains strong! Jabrila will keep her company in the hospital for a few more days. You may not hear from Jane for the next little while as her body works with the challenge of new cells but know she loves hearing from all of you. I love my sisters. They rock!

Detour

The next day I woke to feelings of total wiped-outness. I was beyond tired, the diarrhea came back and I barely could move. My goal of the day was to take a shower. One simple goal and even that seemed taxing. My goddaughter, Yolanda, showed up for a visit, but I was having a hard time communicating. I remember telling her "I can't hold a conversation." She seemed okay with that and chatted with others or just hung out and read. It was sweet that she just wanted to be with me. Shortly after she left, so did my powers to pee. As much as I tried, nothing was happening.

The nurse did an ultrasound which determined my bladder was full, and then used a catheter to expel it. It was supposed to be a one time, quick fix, but ended up going back in almost as soon as it was removed. It remained for two or three days. This was a really low point for me. I'd championed my way through this whole procedure and now the effects of chemo, radiation, and the transplant were taking away my energy, drive, and pride. I felt weak, discouraged, and somewhat helpless.

As a result, I checked out for a few days. I remember very little. In fact when I finally came back to a reality state, I was really surprised at what day it was. I remember only bits and pieces of conversations, walks, procedures. I guess that was a blessing, but maybe not so much for my sister and brother.

Day 7

May 7, 2013

One week ago today Jane received my stem cells. It was a good day, a day of ceremony and moving on. Well that was a good day and since then it has been rough for Jane, really rough. One day she looked up at me and said "I feel like I've been rode hard and put away wet." That just begins to tell you how hard this journey is for her. As I spend the days with her I keep in my mind that all this is so we can all spend more days together and I feel a heart wrenching gratitude for her and her journey for a cure. You won't be hearing from her for a while, just too hard to muster up the energy. One of us will be keeping you all in touch best we can. I am leaving on Thurs. to go home. It is hard to leave....... The doctors keep telling us she is doing well, that this is all to be expected from radiation and chemo therapy. Her blood counts have hit the low mark and today she received her first neupogen shot to kick start stem cell production. Once the stem cells start producing, she should start to feel better. She has lost all her hair, had the last of it shaved by one of her dear nurses. Yes, she has lost her hair, her appetite, and weight, but not her spirit. She still has her buck up pants on and I don't think they will be coming off any time soon.
Her strength is sustained by all your loving words, prayers and

Detour

thoughts. I could never find the words great enough to express how much they all mean to her. Thank you & Happy Trails. Jabrila

I did not leave on Thursday. It was just too hard and Jane told me she wasn't ready for me to go, I stayed. My days start with a visit across the street to the coffee stand where good music and happy faces were always there to greet me. It is a good way to start the day. I always get a scone, blueberry or strawberry, in hopes that Jane would want one. I feel good when she eats something but for now she has no appetite. Her taste buds are not working, so no taste. She is very sensitive to smells, easy to feel nauseated. She has a rash on her neck, back and chest that was very irritating. She could see, but often through a haze of drugs or having blood counts so low, and her entire body was irradiated, so it took too much energy to look. All her senses were not what she was used to. Nothing she was going through was possible to get used to.

And everyday that is what she did. She would get through another day. At night she would often have bad dreams, crazy dreams, which was one of the many side effects of the many medications she was on. We would often talk during the night and early morning. One time Jane told me she felt she was between the worlds. I asked her what world she felt she was heading towards. "Just between" is all she said. I told her I'd like her in the world I was in. We had a moment looking at each other, and then she went to sleep. I sat on my bed, looked out the window, my back to Jane and cried. As I looked at the lights of the city I thought of our life together and did not want it to end. I wanted more time with my sis and more time for her. She told me she had things to do this time around and that she didn't feel done. That was what I was praying for, her life. In the morning after I got my coffee and scone (that she did not eat) she asked if I was crying during the night. Yes, I was having a sad moment but I was fine. And she understood...

Not long after the transplant, after I came back from la la land, one of the doctors came in for my morning check up. I was sitting up in the chair feeling pretty good as he looked over my blood work. His face lit up like a candle and he exclaimed that it was unheard of to see platelet counts come back so fast. This was a very good sign that the cells were taking and beginning to do their job. He actually called me a rock star. That felt pretty good considering I'd felt like a rock only days before.

This continued over the next few days with my counts rising, my platelets cooperating, and adjectives like excellent, amazing, and wow used often. A lot of credit was given to blinotumamab, the antibody used during the clinical trial. It made sense to me. Going into a life altering procedure feeling good has got to have some power behind it. If I had taken the alternate route, more chemo to get into remission, I would have gone to transplant feeling the effects of post chemo. Not such a great feeling. By having almost 5 weeks of remission and benign side effects of the antibody, I was in way better shape to receive this procedure. As I mentioned before, I was allowed the time to prepare physically and mentally, because of the clinical trial.

Now some will disagree and say that the antibody was only a small part, and the true healing came from prayers. I am not in disagreement with this either. Whatever the reason, or combinations of reasons (prayer, good health, positive attitude, antibodies, caring caregivers), my life was coming back strong and quick. I felt uplifted knowing I was the first blinotumamab/transplant person at UCSF, and that it was going so well. It created hope for others, excitement for doctors and nurses, and the success of the transplant brought with it an overall feeling of accomplishment and happiness. I know that doesn't sound very clinical, but happiness is what radiated from all involved. I was grateful for this kind of energy and knew that things were finally looking up.

Hearing words like *excellent, rock star* and *incredible* is not a bad thing when you've just been through six months of questionable everything. I have always been in wonder of the resiliency of my body, but then, it became apparent that with the new stem cells, I was headed off to a very good start.

New cells

May 10, 2013

Well hello. It's a cool foggy day in San Francisco but I am warmed by your lovely messages. I am so blessed by having such great friends

Detour

and family keeping me in their thoughts and prayers and making me laugh. Thank you all for that. The effects of the chemo and total body irradiation were rough to say the least. For about a week I did very little and lay very low. My entire GI track was inflamed, irritated and I'm convinced a little angry. I slept sitting up mostly due to reflux and had crazy nightmarish dreams. My bladder decided to quit working for about 5 days and I developed a rash on my shoulders and back. ...Add to this the feeling of having the stomach flu and....okay, I'll stop now. So that is why you haven't heard from me. I'm so glad you kept in touch, though. Now today is a whole new day. My new cells are grafting and growing like gangbusters. My intestinal problems have reduced significantly and today I was able to walk 5 laps around the hallway. All in all, things are looking up. I will most likely be able to leave the hospital next week! Reflecting on this whole process I am impressed with the resiliency of the human body and what it can withstand. This has been a physical and emotional roller coaster, yet here I am telling you today "I feel good." The next watch sign is graft vs. host disease, which means my new cells reject their new living space. This can happen on different levels at different times, so we're all keeping an eye out for that. Truthfully, I'm not all that concerned. I think my new cells are jumping for joy. I know that I am! I will be in touch and keep you up on the latest adventures of Jane's new cells...Love and good health to you all and many happy trails. Jane

About 4 days before my release, I developed a cough and a runny nose. As protocol warrants, the nurse did a nasal swab to make sure I had no bacterial infection starting. Little did we know at the time the test would take 3 to 4 days and I couldn't leave my room until I was cleared. So finally I'm feeling up to getting out of bed, walking, moving about, and I'm put on lock down. It was kind of shocking. I had a great view, a decent size room, and my sister staying with me, but yikes! I wanted out.

The nurse brought in a stationary bike and that helped, but I really wanted to leave the room. I'd beg the night nurse to allow me to walk the halls when no one was around, but the answer was always, "I'll check that out" and then no response.

During this time I tried to learn to knit, which was a total disaster. Between chemo brain, neuropathy, and general weakness of the body and mind, it turned out to be not so great. Humorous for my sister though. So I crocheted, something I already knew, and read, and watched movies, and looked out the window. I had visitors that kept me occupied, and the nurses were always filling me in on the haps of the outside world, but being in the outside world is what I wanted most.

Detour

Fourteen days after transplant, I was deemed non contagious and hit the floor, not quite running, but so happy to move and walk and get out of my room. After being laid up for so long, it takes a bit to get going again. I thought I was doing great - adrenalin is a wonderful tool for that, but I quickly felt the weakness and slowed down my pace. I was determined to stay out of my room as much as possible. A nurse practitioner called a meeting with me and my family to go over the restrictions of my release. I was to be on house arrest for the next 30 days with little or no contact of the outside world, except bi-weekly visits to the clinic and daily walks outside. I had to be within 30 minutes of the hospital and check in twice a week to the clinic. It seemed more like I was being released from jail than the hospital. Hand washing became an event and gloves and masks were my new fashion apparel.

Despite all this there were bonuses, big bonuses. I was encouraged to get out and walk daily, something I love to do and doing it outside overrode a lot of the other restrictions. I was also not to do housework for the next year (sweet!). No gardening or cleaning up pet poo. Oh and due to certain medications and prevention measures, sun protection was to become my new religion. My sister

Detour

and brother-in-law joined David in packing up from my twenty-one-day adventure at 11 Long, and thank God they were there. Mentally I really thought I was fine and dandy, but getting up and getting organized was a whole other thing. It was crazy difficult. You know when you have the flu and you don't think you're really that sick, so you get up to start a project and have to sit back down? It's kind of like that.

So I let them do it all. I showered and waited for my Picc line to be removed, the last thing before my grand exit. After that it was a 15-minute lie-down followed by discharge paperwork, then freedom. I'd said good-bye to most of the nurses as I walked the halls earlier, so I was able to leave without too much emotion. It's such a bittersweet exit. I'd spent three weeks with these fabulous people who cared for me so deeply, in every sense of the word, and I was leaving them to literally start a new life. A life they helped me begin. Most of them had been my nurses five years before on my first go round, so there was a definite connection there. Gratitude doesn't begin to touch the feelings I developed for the nurses at 11 Long. It went so much deeper. But, it being their job, they all wished me well and said "we don't ever want to see you here again." It was a rejection I embraced.

Release

May 14, 2013

Another beautiful day in San Francisco. The sun is actually out today, and without the fog I can see the towers of the Golden Gate Bridge, the ocean and the bay. It's quite lovely. The best part is that today I get to breathe the fresh air too. It's discharge day! After 22 days I am being released. It sounds like a long time, actually it is a long time, but for an alo-transplant patient (meaning received donor cells) who received total body irradiation, it's remarkable. My doctors are impressed with the quick recovery and especially my platelet count, the indicator that the new cells are engrafting. Outside sounds really good to me right now. This next step is very new to me, nothing I've been through before, but I'll continue moving on forward toward the next step, and then the one after that. In the past few weeks, my brother and his fiancé have been amazing and will continue to help out in many ways. I am so blessed. As always I appreciate your encouragement, humor, and just staying in touch. I love reading your entries. I'll stay in touch as best as I can. Until next time, keep those cards and letters coming in. Enjoy the lovely spring and find something to be grateful for each day; there's a lot out there.
Happy Trails, Jane

Detour

It felt so great to walk down the hall and off the hospital floor. It was the start of something new. And it exhausted me. By the time I was off the elevator, I had to hold onto my sister to steady myself for the walk to the front of the hospital where David was waiting in the car. They allowed me to go without a wheelchair, but Nurse Karen escorted us all the same. I still remember the way it felt to breathe in fresh air. The doors opened and it hit me like a blast. Of course it was San Francisco, on a busy street in a parking roundabout with buses and cars, but still I was outside and headed for a two-day stay next to the ocean.

I am so thankful for people willing to help. I could never have moved from hospital to hotel without my sister Kate and her husband Wendell. Kate pre-cleaned everything, unpacked my bags, shopped for David and me, making it easy for me to lie down and do nothing. Truthfully that was all I could do. I was rather shocked at my weakened condition, so I lay on the bed and watched the three of them bustle around. The room was kind of like a cave, but it was only for two days, then off to Pacifica where we would spend the next four weeks in the camper.

Detour

The following day a home health care nurse showed up to teach us how to run IV Magnesium through my port. Each day I was to have an infusion that took five hours. My brother's fiancé, Robin came too, as a back up in case David wasn't available, or I needed help. The lesson was not rocket science, so it went pretty quickly. Unfortunately it meant for the next five hours, I was tethered once again to an IV pole. It moved clumsily across the carpet, but I could get around. We were on the second floor of the motel, so going out didn't work out too well. I succumbed to watching reruns of NCIS while David worked on the computer then took a walk, and got us some food. The first night we ordered from one of our favorite restaurants in the city and had hamburgers and sweet potato fries. They smelled so great and as I took a bite I savored the texture, and then realized I had an extremely diminished sense of taste. For all the joy and expectation of this wonderful meal, I could not taste it. I worked my way through almost half and then succumbed to a tasteless melancholy.

Over the next two days we tried different infusion schedules so I got some outside walking time in. We usually went into Golden Gate Park to get out of the wind. I used hiking poles or held on to

Detour

David for support. My brand new body felt about 85 years old and my gait didn't disagree. As I hobbled along among the beauty of the park, I couldn't help but feel appreciation for everything. I'd given up, for the most part, feeling sorry for myself or even being angry that I had to go through this whole cancer adventure again. It felt different this time, like the leukemia was really gone for good.

After 2-1/2 days we finally left and made it to our new home away from home: a 1990 Toyota Camper parked in an RV Park in Pacifica. We had a very nice spot next to a grassy area with a small tree. It was basically a parking lot on a cliff, but we could hear the ocean and feel the breezes and the sun shined nicely. The ocean breeze was quite wonderful and being able to get up and walk outside was like heaven. For the first two days. Then the fog came in and the wind. It got pretty tricky to figure out when to get out and walk and when to do the infusion, but we worked out a doable solution. The part that was the most difficult was that it was so damn cold.

The coldest winter I ever spent was the summer I spent in San Francisco. I'm with Mark Twain on that one.

Detour

I went to the clinic twice a week and David would usually find some nice place to walk on the way back. Sometimes we'd walk by the beach, but that was later on. It was a daily ritual though to keep moving, even if it was fifteen minutes in the cold. The good thing about the infusions was it made me rest. I'd usually prop up at the table and read or nap. We no longer had Internet power for movies, so I also played games and checked emails. It kept me from doing too much.

Tom and Robin joined us the following week, renting the space next to us with their RV. It was fun to have some company that was there, but not totally in your face. David had to leave for work for a couple of days, so they took over as caregivers. We often ate meals together and walked. They brought these crazy fun three wheel bicycles that were a blast. Life was starting to feel more normal. Additionally they had their dog Scooby, a mid sized pit bull who loved me. I would go into their camper and sit on the couch when I was really cold and let him lie across me, the ultimate warmth and comfort. The weeks went by and my appointments were all pretty much the same. I'd get blood drawn, vitals taken, and see either Lisa or Dr Martin. Usually it was Lisa. My body reacted quite well to the transplant and I never needed extra blood products or anything. My medicines were monitored, sometimes changed, and we talked about foods with protein and calories, as by now I'd lost about twenty pounds.

Each day David would hook me up for my magnesium infusion and I'd often think this is so not sexy. I wondered what he must be thinking, seeing my body so unfamiliar even to me and having to deal with it so up close and personal on a daily basis. I imagined him going somewhere else in is head, so as not to think too much about it. We did not discuss this, just went through the daily motions of infusion. He was always kind and thoughtful, and I'm grateful for his care. After being hooked up, he'd usually take his mountain bike out for a couple of hours. This was good medicine for both of us, especially David. I had my resting time and he had his active time. It worked out well; plus it gave us both alone time and space.

Once, while looking at my body (up close and personal), David noticed a blackhead on my face and another one on my chest. He went to the drug store to buy those little blackhead remover kits, so I plastered one on my face and one on my chest. I must have not let it set or something because it didn't work. The second time I tried, the face one was gone but the one on my chest remained. I worked on in for another day or two before realizing I was trying to remove the tattoo that marked the radiation line-up spot. I laughed so hard and laughed again when I told David and later my sister Annie. Again, laughter is the best medicine.

The Roughness of Nature

May 22, 2013

I'm sitting in the camper listening to the waves crash, the wind howl and reflecting on the roughness of nature. I tend to think of nature as peaceful and filled with splendor; but it is really tough! It can be loud and discourteous, wild and often hurtful. And then it's balanced with beauty, grace, and inspiration. That's kind of how I'm feeling these days. This journey has been rougher than I ever would have imagined. I'm learning to not be so hard on myself when I have difficulties and discomfort. It's a long, long process and I'm realizing that one day at a time, one step at a time, is what I can manage for now. I'm learning to respect my body and all it is going through. Granted most of the reasons I feel so crappy are chemically induced, but I still believe in the balance of nature and the miracle of new life and cell growth in my body. I am grateful each day for this new chance and use that as a balance when I become overwhelmed. All in all, everything is going well; better than expected for an old lady who received TBI. The docs and nurses are thrilled with my recovery and tell me fatigue is oh so typical and I need to take it easy. That I do. David makes sure I get out on daily walks, even if it means driving away from the coast to where it's not as windy and cold. Speaking of David, he is an amazing caregiver. Each day I have a 5 hour infusion of magnesium, as one of my meds depletes a lot of it. Each day David hooks up the IV, flushes my port, unhooks the IV and flushes again. In addition he cleans, cooks, goes shopping, and does it all with patience and understanding. I am so blessed to have him here with me. It's been a crazy few months for us both, but I find his presence familiar, comforting, and easy. He may have another story to tell.... Maybe I'll have him do the next journal entry. My brother Tommy and Robin have been going ABCD "above and beyond the call of duty" also. They bring me food, do laundry, and are bringing their camper up next week, so David can leave for work. As for the campground, it's really a parking lot on a cliff that looks over the ocean. However, there are lots of places to walk, the air is very fresh, we can hear the ocean, we can walk 100 feet and look out over the ocean for miles, and despite all this, it's very quiet and I am *happy to be here. We've learned to bundle up when we watch the sunset and keep the stampede strings tight on our hats. The camper is small, but I call it cozy. It's all in the wording you know. As I said, all in all everything is going very well. Take care my dear friends and remember to count your blessings. You all are at the top of my list. Happy Trails, Jane*

During our beach time we had few visitors and even fewer sunny nice days. When they happened, we were out walking towards the pier and along the beachfront. Mostly though it was cold. David had an alarm on his phone that rang fifteen minutes before sunset. We'd bundle up each evening and walk to the edge of the cliff and watch as the sun went down. After a couple of weeks, on the really cold and windy nights we'd look at each other and say "Well?" Usually answering, "No I'm good" and go back to what we were doing in the warmth of the camper.

Eventually, the weather warmed up and we enjoyed a sunny windless couple of days. It's amazing how warm 62 degrees feels when the sun is shining and the wind is not blowing. Staying covered up became a challenge. I would slather on 55 sunscreen, wear a hat and gloves, long sleeves and try to stay in the shade. When the sun was warm, however, I would sit in a lawn chair and soak up the warmth, keeping my skin unexposed. Tommy and Robin camped next to us for the week. They brought these crazy recumbent style bicycles that are easy to balance, so I had quite a few opportunities to expand my exercise options and ride.

After 17 days of house arrest, the only inside place I'd gone, besides the camper, is the clinic. My appointments were pretty quick and my energy level went from about 20% of normal to upwards of 60%, I think. Still slow, but moving along. I walked about two miles a day and looked forward to it. During one clinic visit I had time between appointments and decided to walk around near the clinic. I have to say; those hills in SF about did me in! My nurse practitioner said, "Yeah, but you'll have great looking calves." Bonuses, bonuses...

Detour

The warmth didn't last long, and the weather turned cool again and almost unbearable. I found a whole new meaning in "Life's a beach." However, my clinic appointments were going well and the docs were still happy with my progress. I showed no signs of graft vs. host and a lot of things started settling down in my system. I felt stronger daily and was able to do more each day. Again, slow and steady. It works for turtles; it worked for me. I loved living vicariously through the Caring Bridge posts and emails. I read a lot and walked daily, sometimes napped, sometimes played word games on the iPad or played cribbage with David. I was getting a little bored, but I took that as a sign of getting better. I was living simply.

A week before we were scheduled to leave the RV Park, we decided we'd had enough of the cold and went to Vacaville to see my sister, Annie. It was a cool day there, but much nicer than the beach. The three of us were developing these upper respiratory things that wiped us out, so we spent the day just hanging out. I needed to get out of the cold, so the following Saturday, I moved in with Annie in her Vacaville house. That was the plan all along, but we moved it up a couple of days. Never have I enjoyed the heat of a day so much. It was around 100 degrees, and I soaked it in.

Annie's front porch was a delightful shady place to sit and read and talk and eat, so I was there often, only going inside when the heat got too intense.

The day after I moved in, David went home. He was sicker than either Annie or I and remained that way for over a week. It felt so odd knowing he was at home sick and I was 150 miles away not helping him out; another of those "not in my control" times. David returned a week later to switch cars, bringing me my truck, so I could have a vehicle when I was ready to drive. He stayed a very short time, sanitizing everything before he left and drove home sick as a dog. Annie and I recovered shortly, but David's illness kept him down for almost three weeks.

My time at Annie's was wonderfully healing. She would take me to my appointments twice a week, and then we'd take a drive or go somewhere we'd never been. The appointments remained positive and some of the medicines were being cut back. The magnesium infusion was only three hours, and over the next couple of weeks it was tapered down to pills. (That was a glorious day. What freedom!!)

At 50 days, I was officially half way through my 100 days of post transplant care. All was going well, despite the slight set back of the respiratory crud. I delighted in the ability to be outside in the warmer air and relished my time on the front porch. I walked twice a day, before it got hot and in the evening just as the sun set. I love being outside and sitting in the sun, but I was not about to break the rules after everything my body had gone through, so I wore long sleeves, long pants, and a big sun hat. I always sported 50spf sunscreen and sometimes wore gloves. I missed tank tops and shorts, so I wore those while being a dog in the house on hot days.

Detour

My energy level was up and down. I napped daily and rejoiced in being barefoot and bareheaded. I began some meditation again too. I found I wasn't very good at it but having some time each day to sit in stillness is really good for my medicine head. My brain was all over the place, much as a result of the medications I was taking. It felt good to relax and focus on just my breath, or try to clear my head and not think. I tend to over think, so it was a challenge, but I usually felt more relaxed and peaceful when done. Annie shopped for me and I helped out with cooking and doing dishes, which were not on my restrictions list. Life was feeling more normal.

I was really grateful she'd taken me in. There's no place like home, but Annie's was pretty close, the bonus being Cody, her black lab. He was very good company. It was so comforting to be in the company of the big black blob, as we kindly refer to him. He taught me to be a dog. Take a walk, take a nap. Eat something, take a nap. Lie down for a minute, take a nap. Annie left at one point for ten days, so it was just me and Cody. Robin came by occasionally and when I had an appointment someone from my family would come and take me, usually staying overnight.

Detour

Otherwise it was Cody and me. It had been a long time since I'd been alone, on my own, and it felt really good. It was a nice break after being so thoughtfully cared for for months, to be on my own. I had back up people close at hand if I needed something, so I was in total comfort. During this time, I did have the pleasure of a visit from my niece Noora. She told me that people are healthier when they take deep breaths, stay hydrated, and move. I couldn't agree more. She is a massage therapist and knows a lot about the body. I benefitted from her knowledge with two leg massages. I could not believe the difference she made. My knees were sore, my balance off, and my legs felt heavy. The massage was relaxing and a tiny bit painful, but afterwards I felt like a new person. Like my spirit was renewed. There's something to be said for increased circulation. It didn't hurt to have the loving hands of a great massage therapist either.

But for the most part, it was just Annie and me. It had been a very long time since I had a roommate besides David, and I must say Annie was a wonderful roommate. Time spent with her was relaxing and fun. She left me alone when I was feeling yucky, shopped for me, and took me on drives to get us both out of the house.

Illumination

Jun 26, 2013

There are flowers in my sister's yard that seem luminescent. The bright yellow in contrast to the black is amazing. They look as if they might glow in the dark. I am so enjoying the summer flowers here and feel myself perking up daily, reaching upwards towards the sun, and growing...metaphorically of course. My spirits are raised though and I am feeling illuminated by my continued progress, the world around me, and the loving support of friends and family. Sounds corny, but all this does brighten my day. I saw the doctor yesterday and he used the word excellent many times. That's a nice word to hear from a medical professional. I asked him if he was going to let me go early, since I was doing so well, but he said no. Just a simple, yet meaningful no. I always have to try. So it looks like I'll be going home in early August. In the meantime, he is going to start cutting back on some of my daily meds. Yay! Hopefully that will include the IV magnesium. I am down to only a 3 hour infusion daily, so that's progress. My sister has been taking me on these very cool adventures. We explored Mare Island, an old navy shipyard and munitions plant that has a beautiful walking area right near the Carquinez Straits and the Napa River. We also drove to Lake Berryessa along Putah Creek. She loves it, and I love going. My friend Beth came to spend last weekend here and we all had a wonderful time. Especially Cody, the lab, who Beth pampered with doggie massages. So life is moving along well. I hope you are enjoying summer and finding time to take good care of yourselves. There is nothing like an early morning or late evening summer walk. It's the best. Take care of yourselves and each other. Think of you often. Thanks for keeping in touch. Jane

Time passed slowly as I gained strength daily. I lived on toast, ice cream, and vegetables. Strange diet, but it worked. Annie ate a lot of veggies and I could eat some. Others were too hard on my still very sensitive digestive system. I usually tried to add a meat or rice to our evening meal and I often cooked. Shortly after my magnesium infusion I often felt lightheaded and off balance. Annie and I scientifically (meaning we discussed this and came to our own conclusion) decided that I should eat something fatty while getting the infusion. Hence, my ice cream diet. I was low on weight, so that didn't matter and what a great excuse to indulge. The funny thing is prior to the transplant ice cream was a sort of take it or leave it option. During this time it was a "can't wait to see Ben and Jerry" lifestyle.

I was restricted from doing housekeeping, but totally able to cook a meal and clean up the kitchen. It was a very slow process, but I didn't have much else to do. One day I decided to make broccoli salad, as I couldn't eat deli food that had been sitting out. I got my friend Sue's recipe and Annie bought the ingredients. I started cooking the bacon and then I'd sit back down to rest. I'd chop onions and broccoli and then go rest. It took almost all day to make what I referred to as "10 hour broccoli salad."

That's how my life went, slow and steady, but feeling a little better each day. Some days I would have to force myself to get off the couch and take a walk, but on those days I would celebrate making it around the block, or even to the corner and back. In the evenings Annie and I would often meditate together, which was very relaxing and good for my soul. I felt a sense of Spirit coming back in and was almost overwhelmed with gratitude. We listened to podcasts that reflected goodness and ways toward positive living and healing. I began feeling a stronger sense of self.

On the 4th of July, Annie and I ventured to a couple of small towns on the delta, winding up near a boat ramp. We spent a little time throwing sticks in the water for Cody, who loved it and then I offered to drive home. I thought "Hey, it's Independence Day; let's honor that." So I got in Annie's stick shift car and headed home. My brain was pretty clear and there wasn't much traffic, so off we went with me in the driver's seat. There was something awesome about engaging in a task that up until then had seemed too complicated and quite frankly dangerous. I was coming back. I was celebrating my independence in an ordinary, yet significant way. And it felt wonderful.

I enjoyed the company of friends and family who would visit to take me to appointments, and I enjoyed my solitude. For my birthday, David took me to Nevada City to visit friends. Driving there was the same direction as heading home. I realized just how homesick I had become. I loved staying with Annie, but had a reality check while driving towards Reno. I thought of my animals, my friends, my home. It had been so long since I had been home; I had lost sight of it. Heading towards Reno reminded me of my "other life," the one I'd left behind all this time. I wondered what being home would be like. Was I the same person who left? As we curved through the mountain roads toward Nevada City I felt at peace, the kind of peace only the mountains bring me. I was ready to go home, but after all this time away, knew I could easily handle a couple more weeks.

Detour

After returning to Vacaville, Tom and Robin came by for birthday pizza. My god-daughter, Yolanda, and her family also stopped in for a quick happy birthday visit where she surprised me with plane tickets to Portland in October. This was another reminder of future possibilities and thoughts of the future.

In late July, I was at an appointment at UCSF. Annie dropped me off and went adventuring around Golden Gate Park, as the appointments usually took two to three hours. As I was leaving I heard someone mention Chad's mom. I became alert and asked if they meant Chad Hickey, my old friend from 11 Long. Yes, that was him and that was when I learned he had passed away the month before due to complications of graft vs. host. I knew he had been struggling and hadn't heard from him since April, but the news was pretty harsh. When Chad first told me he was out of remission, I felt a huge case of survival guilt. Why was I doing so well, when others were experiencing such major set backs and even dying? I wanted to honor them by staying as healthy as I could, but the sadness and remorse was difficult. I tried a cancer support group for a while, but found that each week everyone hashed over their illnesses and side effects. That wasn't quite what I was looking for. So I moved forward and never really dealt with the feelings.

I knew he was in bad shape from the GVH, and I feel it's a blessing when someone is released from such intense suffering. I think he watches over me sometimes, challenging me to be stronger than the disease, to make it for all of them. His last four text messages are still on my cell phone. I can't seem to erase them. I've dreamt about him, that I was in the hospital awaiting discharge and he was visiting. He looked pretty good except for the sores on his arms. In my dream I remember thinking, I'm glad he's not dead. I heard he was, but he's not and he's here to help me through this. I was truly saddened at the thought of never talking with him again.

My husband's response to the news of Chad's passing was "It's time to celebrate your life." Good advice.

Detour

On August 5th, 98 days after my transplant I had a bone marrow biopsy, to make sure there were no cancer cells growing. My sister Annie went with me and babysat afterwards in my Percocet/adivan stupor. I went back to her house and slept the afternoon away. Later, she made me macaroni and cheese, and I realized that indeed it was a comfort food. My appointments were now changed to weekly, so. I did not need to return to UCSF until the 13th.

Feeling independent and fine to drive, the next day, 99 days after my transplant and 1 day short of "100 days", I decided to leave. There had been so many detours along the past 6+ years, but, here I was, finally on the final stretch, this long, straight shot home.

I left Annie's in the late morning and cried as I drove through Vacaville. I already missed her and Cody, but I was heading home with "Celebrate Good Times" playing on the radio. Talk about a moment. The drive home offered lots of time for reflection, which I did on the entire drive. What a journey. What a ride. I knew what it meant to survive. Literally, the definition of Survive is to remain alive or in existence. Continue life or activity. To live, exist, or remain active beyond the extent of; outlive.

Detour

Outlive what? Surviving is so much more than remaining alive, and doing it longer than others. Was I a survivor just because I outlived Ron and Chad and DeEtta? Survival value includes a quality possessed by an organism, *quality* being the operative word.

Attitude is what kept me alive. It came in many forms – an attitude of gratitude believe it or not. I wasn't exactly grateful for being hospitalized with leukemia, but I made gratitude my spiritual practice when nothing else came to me. I was grateful to be in a caring environment, to be surrounded by the love of family and friends, to be prayed for and thought of in a good light, for the ability to withstand the treatments, for the treatments themselves, for good health insurance, a supportive husband and loving friends willing to care for my home and animals while I was gone. I truly had so much to be grateful for.

It wasn't always positive, but I tried – I would continue to try – to keep negative thinking out of my way. I blessed everything and wouldn't listen to anyone with "poor Jane" in his or her voice. An attitude of "this too shall pass," during the rough times coupled with living each moment with awareness and learning not to judge these moments is how I learned mindfulness. It's how I survived.

Detour

I arrived home, pulled into the garage and again cried. I couldn't get out of my truck, as I felt paralyzed with gratitude and relief. My emotions were definitely a roller coaster of activity. When I did get out, I went out back to greet my horses I hadn't seen since April, then went and spent an hour just sitting on the couch absorbing the gladness of being home. It felt strangely like I never left.

Yet as I sat I considered the latest lessons learned:

Become your own best friend. Loving oneself is very helpful.

Trust the process; things don't always work out the way you think they should, but for me they worked out in spite of myself.

Life goes on – the world didn't stop because I had a cancer diagnosis. My world changed significantly, but others' lives simply went on, as they should.

Change is not a bad thing.

Going with the flow is much easier than trying to control situations you have limited control over.

Keep your family and friends close, but allow them to process as they need to.

Give yourself space and time to be alone with your thoughts and reactions.

Detour

Find the person or people you are most comfortable talking with and let them hear you.

Discovering who you really are can be powerful and healing.

Judgment is overrated. Acceptance is healing. Forgiveness allows one to move forward.

As the day progressed I relaxed in the comfort of being home. David came home from a hike a bit later and together we sat in the backyard, contemplating our new beginning.

Detour

Special Thanks

"Gratitude is the heart's memory"

I have always had a very good memory and a big heart. Gratitude has opened my heart like nothing else ever has. I would like to acknowledge the staff at both University of California at San Francisco and the City of Hope, whose loving care and support gave this journey a gentler path. Thank you Dr. Martin, Lauren, and Lisa from UCSF for hanging in there with me, giving me the confidence to continue treatment, and for saving my life. And thank you to Dr. Stein from City of Hope for including me in the clinical trial. My most special thanks go to some very important people in my life to whom I am eternally grateful.

My twin sister, stem cell donor, and best friend, Jabrila; without you my life would be so very different. I may not even be here. Thank you for your love, support, laughter, and of course your super power cells. Thank you for the contributions you made to this book and thank you Wali for supporting Jabrila's decision to spend so much time with me.

Detour

My sister Annie: for being the best roommate ever! And for always being there to listen, share, eat, drive, and go on adventures. Thanks to Cody, for teaching me how to be a dog.

My sister Kate: for taking such good notes, always being available, and making what seemed impossible, possible. You are the wind beneath my wings…

My brother Tom and his fiancé Robin: for camping out in the cold with us, appearing late at night to show you care, for going above and beyond with helpfulness. And for bringing Scooby to the coast to keep me warm.

My nieces Kachina, Noora and Hannah and my goddaughter Yolanda: for being a wonderful support system to me.

My dear friend Beth: for standing guard with your humor, sensibility and lovely spirit

Nancy: for always being there to comfort and humor me; not to mention shuttle me back and forth to the city.

Deb, Mike, and Linda: for taking care of everything important in my life while I was not able to.

Thank you Jessica, for editing this book, offering such helpful comments, and assisting in getting it ready for publishing.

Last, but not least, to David, my soul mate, other best friend, and love of my life. It's been a rough road, but you smoothed it out in so many ways. Thank you for giving me the chance to grieve without judgment and cry on your shoulder when I was trying so hard to be brave. Thanks for giving me hope and hanging in there. You proved yourself as caregiver extraordinaire, dedicated chauffer, and keeper of my sanity. I appreciate you more than you will ever know.

Resources

Here are a few resources I found very helpful:

American Cancer Society – www.cancer.org 1-800-227-2345

Anti-Cancer Club www.anticancerclub.com

A wonderful website filled with great information

BeTheMatch.org – National Marrow Donor Program

Caring Bridge – www.caringbridge.org

This website is an amazing way to keep in touch and share information with many family and friends at the same time.

City of Hope www.cityofhope.org

1500 East Duarte Ave

Duarte, CA 91010

1-800-826-HOPE

Leukemia and Lymphoma Society www.lls.org

National office: 1311 Mamaroneck Ave. Suite 310

White Plaines, NY 10605

1-800-955-4572

UCSF Medical Center – www.ucsfhealth.org

505 Parnassus Ave.

San Francisco, CA 94143

415-476-1000

About the Author:

Jane Wirth lives in Reno, Nevada with her husband David and her two, 4 legged friends; Velvet, a 23 yr old Morgan horse, and Franklin the turtle, a 15+ year old red-eared slider. She is currently in remission and continues post transplant immunotherapy. This is her first published work.

Contact Jane at: Detour2HappyTrails@gmail.com

Made in the USA
San Bernardino, CA
11 June 2015